D0480274

Golf Stories

GOLF
STORIES

BY GERALD BATCHELOR

WITH FORTY-FIVE ILLUSTRATIONS
BY E. W. MITCHELL

BLOOMSBURY

LONDON • NEW DELHI • NEW YORK • SYDNEY

Published by Bloomsbury Publishing Plc
50 Bedford Square
London WC1B 3DP
www.bloomsbury.com

First published 1914 by A&C Black
This facsimile edition published 2013

ISBN: 978-1-4081-8261-1 (hardback)
ISBN: 978-1-4081-8263-5 (EPub)

A CIP catalogue record for this book is available from the British Library.

ACKNOWLEDGEMENTS

Cover and internal illustrations © E. W. Mitchell

This book is produced using paper that is made from wood grown in managed, sustainable forests. It is natural, renewable and recyclable. The logging and manufacturing processes conform to the environmental regulations of the country of origin.

Printed and bound in the UK by CPI Group (UK) Ltd, Croydon, CR0 4YY

10 9 8 7 6 5 4 3 2 1

For permission to reprint the contents of this book my grateful acknowledgments are due to the Editors and Proprietors of *Golf Illustrated*, *The World of Golf*, *The Golf Monthly*, and *Golfing*. I would also thank the Proprietors of *Golf Illustrated* for permission to use some of the illustrations which have appeared in that paper.

GERALD BATCHELOR

CONTENTS

CONTENTS

GOLF STORIES

Foozle's Philosophy

" **F**ORE " warned is forearmed.

'Tis better to have lost and paid than never to have played at all.

Charity begins at the home hole.

Once a scoffer, always a golfer.

Faint heart never won fair stymie.

The surly word matches the worm.

Up all night, down all day.

Don't try to run before you can pitch.

Putt in haste and repent at leisure.

The best-placed bunkers are those which we never fail to carry.

Even a wormcast will turn the ball unless trodden on.

Spare the turf and spoil the mashie shot.

The hole is greater than a half.

Never look a gift hole in the mouth.

'Tis a bad start that gives no chance of recovery.

'Tis more blessed to give than to receive advice from a caddie.

When two players are looking for a ball it is easy to discover which of them has lost it.

A player may willingly receive tips from his caddie.

A caddie will willingly receive tips from a player.

Tis a short putt that has no terrors.

The longer the grass the shorter the temper.

Little pitches have great cares.

A good putt needs no push.

A man may smile and smile, and be a loser.

Too many landlords spoil the course.

None but the brave deserve the fairway.

Faith may remove mountains, but when the ball buried in a molehill it is safer to take a niblick to it.

A foozler and his ball are not soon parted.

Never lean too much on one club, or it may one day let you down.

A pitch in time saves nine, in the bunker.

'Tis an ill win that blows nobody any good.

The early starter catches the wormcasts.

He's an unwise pro. that beats his only pupil.

A stroke deferred maketh the onlookers sick.

Give a caddie a bad name, but don't d——n him.

A little local knowledge is a dangerous thing.

A high ball gathers no mud—till it drops.

A pot-hunter makes no profit in his own club.

First catch your Scotsman—then beat him.

Nature is a hard taskmistress—to beat.

People in glass houses shouldn't live near golf-links.

A good line is that which has length, strength, but no wildness.

One good shot with a driver makes the whole world keen.

The more we try to win, the harder it is to lose.

Cross bunkers make cross players.

Take care of the club and the ball will take care of itself.

You've got to get down if you want to be "up," and you've got to be up to get down.

There's many a good putt played in jest.

Unbecoming events cast their shadows behind them.

One good shot will not win a medal.

Tyros run in where champions can't get dead.

A fellow failing makes one wondrous kind.

Fools make bets for their betters to profit by.

Self-possession is nine points of the game. To make a good stroke under difficulties is good, but to make a good stroke *over* them is better.

Never twit a man when he's down.

You may know a man's play by the clubs that he carries.

The perfect golfing temperament consists in pretending that you don't mind if you're beaten and don't deserve it if you win.

It is better to be able to hit the ball without knowing how it is done, than to know how it should be done and then make a foozle.

All holes are blind to those who cannot play.

Why carry a putter? Why not hole out with the approach?

It is easy to say " Hard luck ! " when your opponent misses a short putt that gives you the match.

A divot is replaced much more carefully after a good shot than after a bad one.

Least said soonest ended.

Never say " Dead."

The Four-Ball

ON my arrival here early this morning I found a telegram from my cousin to say that he would not be able to play until the afternoon. I failed to get a game, but thinking that there would be a better chance of wiping out my late defeat at Westward Ho! if I could gain some knowledge of Jack's favourite course, I decided to try conclusions with "Colonel Bogey," who is always ready to start. Four men had taken up their position on the tee before me.

"Let's have a four-ball," said the Mathematician. (I invented names to suit them.)

"Right," said the Pot-hunter.

"What is it?" asked the Fat Man.

"Don't you know?" said the Money-grubber. "Why, it's much better than a foursome. More fun for your money, you know. It's quite easy to explain. We play partners, as in Bridge; you and I, say, against Pots and Maths. Whoever does the best score wins the hole for his side. Then if one is out of it, he leaves it to the other. For instance, if you——; but you'll soon see how it works out when we start."

In each of these players I recognised a type un-

7

happily by no means rare in Golf Clubs at the present day.

The Mathematician seemed to regard the game merely as an agreeable excuse for working out abstruse problems. He crept round the links poring over card and pencil, and relinquished them with obvious reluctance when his turn came to play.

The Pot-hunter was one of those selfish players who think only of their own game and of the low score which they hope to accomplish—and to talk about.

The Fat Man represented those who play simply for the sake of exercise, beating a ball along without any apparent object, anxious to reduce their weight rather than their handicap.

The Money-grubber, on the other hand, was certainly interested in the result of the game, but this keenness was probably to be attributed to the fact that he had "a ball on" with each of his opponents. While things went well for his side this man never ceased to talk in a loud and swaggering tone.

"You start off," he said, turning to Fatty ; then, as the latter was addressing the ball, "Mind that ditch on the right there, and be sure to clear the gorse. I always play for a pull here so as to—ah ! topped it badly ! What did I tell you ? Well, I'll see what *I* can do. . . . Lor, what a slice ! Mark it, Fatty, for goodness sake mark it, man. Did you see where it landed ?"

" No," said Fatty ; " you said you were playing for a pull, so I was looking the other way."

" Come on, partner," said Potts, " I think we can do a bit better than that."

But in spite of a terrific swing, he only sent the ball hopping into the long grass.

" Putting at the wrong end," announced the caddie, who seemed privileged to make sarcastic remarks unrebuked, in return for doing duty for all the players. " Good mashie shot," he added, as Maths hit his drive high in the air. Then the party moved forward, and the hunt began.

Those who found their balls went on and holed out, each man playing without any regard to the position of the others. Thus the four, during their race to the green, spread out in a formation highly dangerous to all except the man in the extreme rear.

This point of vantage was usually occupied by Maths, who constantly halted to work out the score, meanwhile forgetting where his ball had gone to.

The others, after finishing the hole, returned to look for Maths' ball, and if it were found its owner was informed what score he had to beat.

On one occasion Fatty displayed such carelessness in addressing his putt that Grubber said, " Careful, now, partner ; you have this for it."

" Don't talk on the stroke," said Fatty, as he missed it ; " you put me off."

" Well, but you must be careful," said Grubber ; " you're

not playing for yourself alone, remember. I've got money on this game."

As may be imagined, the "Colonel" and I did not progress very fast under the circumstances, but as I wanted to finish the round I lit a pipe at the turn and sat down for twenty minutes to let the four-ball go well ahead. At the twelfth tee, however, I again overtook them.

Fatty, who was lying on his back half asleep, was asking, "How do we stand now ?"

"All I know is that I am two under fives to here," said Pots ; "might do rather a good round, I think."

"Let's see," said Maths, eagerly producing his calculations once again, "I'm two down to you, and eight up on Grubber, and all square with Pots, while Pots is three up on——"

"No, no," said Grubber, "you must only reckon as *sides*. How do we stand in the four-ball ?"

"Oh," said Maths, "I'll work that out in a minute. Wait a bit——"

At last the game got moving again, only to meet with another long delay on account of Grubber's losing a ball.

The other three went on, and I played a ball which landed close to where Grubber was standing.

He picked it up ; then, seeming to notice me for the first time, called out, "Is this your ball, sir ?"

"Yes," I said.

"What are you playing with ?" he asked.

"A 'Colonel,'" I replied.

"That's funny, so am I," he said, "and I'm sure this is mine because of this mark which——"

I was saved further discussion by the arrival of Pots, who returned to announce that he had played with Grubber's ball by mistake, and had lost it, as well as his own.

"Horrid nuisance," he went on, "that has spoilt my round, and I was doing quite a good score, too ! Well, that makes you dormy, so here's the ball we had on the game. It will make up for the one you've lost. I've had enough of this and shall walk in now. Rotten bad luck, losing a ball like that. I don't suppose I shall ever do such a good round again !"

The two marched off towards the Club House, arguing about their bets, and were soon followed by Fatty, who said he had "worked up quite a respectable thirst."

Maths, left to finish the four-ball by himself, persevered to the end, accompanied by the caddie's oft-repeated ejaculation, "Glorious Devon ! " in reference to the chunks of that county which Maths removed (but did not replace) at almost every stroke.

When he eventually finished, some three hours after starting, he had accumulated a mass of figures sufficient to exercise his mind for several days without giving him the trouble of walking round the links.

So the four-ball fizzled out.

If the Beasts played Golf

MAN is a selfish brute. He wants to keep all the good things to himself. For many years Scotsmen guarded the secret of the pleasures of golf, and when this secret at last leaked out to England and quickly ran over the whole world, man still tried to monopolise the links.

Once having tasted the blood of a foozled drive, however, his womenfolk and children insisted on sharing his new-found troubles and triumphs. Man has now recognised their right to golf. Should he not extend this concession to the other animals?

Perhaps he would be more inclined to do so if it could be proved that this course would be directly to his advantage.

We have been told that other beasts besides man need recreation of mind as well as body if they are to be brought to their proper state of physical perfection. It is found that sheep which are kept fully occupied and amused show their gratitude by providing a superior quality of mutton. That is why sheep are so often turned loose upon the golf links.

Chickens, also, may be induced to offer a more tender tribute to the taste of man if they are given some real interest in life—such as playing "last across" on some popular motoring high road.

What need of further instances ?   Go to the Zoo, and you will find all the inmates either fast asleep or playing games.   Special appliances are provided for their diversion, but the management have so far shown a lamentable lack of local knowledge in failing to offer adequate opportunities for the playing of golf.

Perhaps it may be doubted that the animals *could* play golf.   Let us see.   You give your dog a stick or a ball to play with, but you never give him *both*.

Many of the poor brutes are evidently designed by nature for the enjoyment of golf.   One or two examples should suffice to prove the point.

The horse often goes out for a long drive.   Sometimes, however, he is inclined to pull a bit, and consequently receives a good many strokes.

The donkey also takes a lot of beating in a team match.   One of his favourite courses is " Ye Banks and Brays."

The pig is a very porky player, and none knows better how to negotiate a sty-mie.

The bat has the good fortune to enjoy a good lie all through the winter.

The tortoise is a slow player, yet we cannot hope to teach him as much as he has taught us.

The cat can quickly come down to scratch.   She can knock spots out of the leopard, anyway.

Most of the fishes get along swimmingly.   The lobster, for instance, is quite good at a pinch, though it must be confessed that he is a confirmed pot-hunter.

The salmon begins life as a "par" player and can always be relied on to keep his plaice. Everyone must have noticed that the sardine has a happy knack of finding the tin.

Some of the animals would, unfortunately, be rather unpopular in the Club house, for who would care to pal up with the long-tailed tit, the lyre bird, the badger, the boar, the grouse, the puff-adder, the cheetah, the carp, or the bear (with a sore head)?

On the ladies' course we should find the spoonbill, and possibly the shrew. The wry-neck would be noticed on the green, and all the game birds would certainly be bittern with the sport.

The secretary bird would be there, closely associated with the dormy mouse and the casual water-rat.

Not to try the reader's indulgence too severely, we may conclude by reminding him that the albatross keeps going all the time, that the rabbit can run down the hole from any distance, that the sand-hopper and the mud-skipper skilfully avoid the bunkers, that the gnu could play quite well if he only newt, that sea-urchins make good caddies, and that the butterfly is frequently found to be dead on the pin.

A " One-Ball " Match

IT was the first day of Spring and I arrived early on the links, eager to make the most of my holiday.

I found a solitary figure in the smoking-room, poring over the latest book on golf, and recognised him as a fellow member whom I knew to be a good golfer, a good sportsman, and one of the pleasantest men in the Club.

Clerkson had retired early from Government service owing to ill-health, and it was understood that, in spite of being an unmarried man, he possessed hardly sufficient means to be able to afford the luxury of playing golf regularly.

"Hullo, Clerkson!" I said, "I haven't seen you here for ages. Have you been away?"

"No," he replied, "I—er—I've given up golf."

"Given up golf?" I repeated in amazement, "*you*, the keenest player in all ——, but you've been ill, perhaps?"

"Yes, I have," he said, "but that is not the real reason. The fact is, I found the game too expensive. I don't complain of my limited income—it is nobody's business but my own—but I don't mind telling you that many a time when I have played here and lost a ball I have been forced to economise by going without my lunch!

"Now you will understand why I have always been so anxious to avail myself of the full five minutes allowed for search, however hopeless the case might appear. It's my own fault for ever taking up golf. I wish I hadn't. No, I don't wish that, and I would willingly deny myself anything rather than be compelled to give it up.

"The limit came when they put up the price of balls. That extra sixpence meant everything to me, you see, so I had no choice but to depart from my earthly paradise.

"I thought I could do it, too, but I was wrong. The exercise of brain and muscle, so happily combined, had become as necessary to me as food and sleep.

"My health began to suffer. Doctors could do nothing. They failed to diagnose my case. I got worse and worse, until I was almost given up.

"This morning I took the matter out of their hands, for I had thought of a plan. I jumped out of bed, enjoyed a big breakfast, and hurried up to the links. I feel better already."

"Excellent!" I exclaimed, "will you have a match?"

"I should be ashamed to ask you to play with me," he replied, "for I'm afraid I might spoil your game."

"What do you mean?" I asked. "You are a better golfer than I am."

"Ah, but I fear you do not quite understand the conditions under which I am compelled to play," he said ; "in future I shall always have to play *without a ball !*"

"Without a ball ?" I repeated ; "you are surely joking. How is it possible ?"

"Well, if you really don't object to watching the experiment," said Clerkson, "I will show you."

"Perhaps you will remember," he continued, as we made for the first tee, "that it is my custom to take a trial swing before every drive ? It was this which suggested the idea. I was always able to judge fairly accurately by the feeling of the swing whether the stroke would have been successful. Will you take the honour ?"

"Shall we have a ball on ?" I asked as usual, forgetting for the moment the peculiar conditions of the coming match. Clerkson seemed to be engaged in a mental struggle. Then he answered "Yes !"

I made a fair drive and stood aside to see what my opponent would do. He took some sand, pinched it into a tee, addressed it carefully, and played.

"Ah !" he exclaimed : "I was afraid I should slice. I must have been standing that way."

He made off towards the rough, where I saw him play two strokes, and we walked on together to my ball. I also played two more shots before reaching the green.

"Where are you ?" I asked.

"Didn't you see it ?" said Clerkson. "I was rather surprised that you did not compliment me on the stroke. It was a wicked lie."

" Are you—are you near the hole ? " I inquired, as I settled down to a long putt.

" I don't see it at present," he replied, looking about, " I hope it hasn't run over.—Good Heavens ! " he went on, as he reached the pin, " It's *in the hole !* " He stooped and seemed to pick it out.

" I really must apologise for that fluke," my opponent said, as we walked to the next tee, " but I knew it was a fine shot directly I had played it, and I thought it deserved to be pretty close."

" It looks as if this were going to be rather a one-sided match," I said to myself, as I watched him dispatch what he described as a " screamer," and I began to wonder whether Clerkson had planned this game in order to provide himself with the necessary ball. Knowing him to be a thoroughly good fellow, however, I dismissed the suspicion from my mind.

These misgivings prevented me from concentrating my attention entirely on the game, with the result that I played very indifferently and reached the second green three strokes to the bad. After I had holed my putt, Clerkson kept walking up and down the green in his attempts to get into the hole.

" Your hole ! " he cried at last ; " putting was always my weak point."

The game continued to be very even. If I obtained a lead of one hole my opponent invariably seemed to hit a tremendous distance from the next tee. At the fourth he played a shot which must easily have

I watched him dispatch what he
described as a "screamer"

beaten the record drive. On the other hand, if he happened to become one up he lost the next by taking three or four putts.

At the sixth hole his ball disappeared into a gorse bush. Formerly he would have been much disturbed by such an occurrence, but now he seemed to accept the situation with philosophic calm.

" Come along ; never mind," he said, after a casual look round ; " it's of no consequence ; only an old gutta, you know.   I'll drop another "—which he did. He must have lost quite half a dozen balls during the round.

At the ninth we were all square. I was beginning to find my game better now.

" Mark it ! " cried Clerkson, directly after driving from the tenth tee ; " I've lost it in the sun."

" I see it." I said ; " you've pulled it rather badly, I'm afraid, and it has landed in ' Purgatory ' bunker." I pointed out to him that it was lying in a hopeless position, and he gave up the hole.

At the twelfth hole Clerkson made a very serious error of judgment. I was diligently looking for his wild drive when I happened to stumble on a brand-new " Dunlop."

" What are you playing with ? " I asked.

" Let me see," he said, watching my face very intently ; " was it a ' Colonel,' or a ' Zodiac,' or a ' Silver King,' or—oh, I know ; it was a ' Challenger.' "

I put the ball in my pocket.

At the fourteenth, where Clerkson had the honour, some workmen were walking across the fairway, quite three hundred yards ahead.

" Do you think I can reach them ? " my opponent asked. I thoughtlessly said, " No, of course not." Directly he had driven he yelled " Fore ! " at the top of his voice. The men looked round.

" That was a narrow escape," he gasped.

" But surely you were a long way short," I said.

" Short ! " he exclaimed, " why, man, it was *right over their heads !* "

He gave me a rare fright at the next.

I had a splendid tee shot, for once, and Clerkson walked straight up to my ball.

" This is mine, I believe," he said.

" Certainly not," I cried, " I am playing with a ' Kite '. "

" *So am I !* " said he.

Fortunately I was able to point out a private mark which I had made on my ball.

We were all square at the eighteenth. I drove out of bounds.

" Did you get a good one ? " I asked anxiously, after he had played.

" A perfect peach," he replied.

I concluded that I had lost the match. I persevered, however, and was playing two more with my approach, while he (so I was informed) was less than a yard from the hole. My mashie shot looked like going in, but the ball came to rest on the edge of the tin.

Clerkson walked up, looked at the ball, went on one knee, then suddenly dashed his cap on the ground in disgust.

" Anything wrong ? " I inquired.

" Wrong ? " he repeated. " Can't you see that you have laid me *a dead stymie ?* "

He studied the line with great care.

" I think there is just room to pull round," he muttered.

He played, and watched, with an agonised expression, the course of his invisible ball.

Suddenly there came a strong puff of wind, and my ball toppled into the hole.

" D——n it all," cried Clerkson, " *I've knocked you in !* "

He picked up my ball, and with it, apparently, his own.

" A halved match," he said, "and I must thank you for an exceedingly interesting game."

I was due in London that evening, and on my return, some weeks later, I learnt that Clerkson had been laid up with a form of brain fever.

Parodies

[*After Thomas Moore*]

THE caddie boy to the links has gone,
In the rotters' ranks you'll find him.
His master's bag he has girded on,
And he stamps the turf behind him.

Oh verdant sward all sclaffed and scarred
By those who wear and tear thee.
One watchful eye the turf shall guard,
One healing sole repair thee !

[*After Kirke White*]

'Tis not the thought of what I owe
That makes this silent tear to flow.
I'd only be too proud to pay
The penalty for my good play.
'Tis this—that I was all alone,
So no one *saw* me hole in one.

24

[*After H. Vaughan*]

Happy those early days when I
Played golf in all simplicity :
Before the links, by Nature made,
Were hacked and scarred by pick and spade ;
Before I'd heard of Bogey, or
Of playing simply for one's score ;
When men preferred to fight for fun,
Rather than what was to be won :
And scorned to use a rubber pill
To counteract their lack of skill.
Let others play their " standard " game :
To me 'twill never be the same.

[*After Coleridge*]

Tell me on what holy ground
May content and peace be found ;
Free from Suffragette surprise,
Safely hid from prying eyes,
From the Public's curious gaze,
From the latest social craze ?
Peace was to be found, of yore,
On the Golf links ; now no more.

D

[*After Byron*]

A golfer to his driver :

Roll on, thou whitened lump of rubber, roll !
Ten thousand d——s sweep over thee in vain ;
In twice ten bunkers have I paid *thy* toll ;
I swear I'll never play with thee again !
Curs'd be the day when thou to me wast lent,
Would I had straight return'd thee unto Brown,
Or lost thee, when I drove into the bent ;
I had not then return'd a " thirteen down."
For all thy failings thou canst ne'er atone ;
Thy faults are thine, thy virtues all my own.

[*After Shelley*]

A golfer to his putter :

I arise from dreams of thee,
Having spent a restless night.
Now at last I learn with glee,
How to put my putting right ;
I arise from dreams of thee,
But when I begin to play,
All my putts, it seems to me,
Like my dreams, have gone astray.

[*After Stoke Poges*, where a team of ladies was defeated
  by a team of gentlemen, who conceded "a half"]

> Try no more, ladies, try no more ;
> Despite your best endeavour,
> You must confess that, by the score,
> Men are (by half) too clever.
> But sigh not so, my fairest foe,
> In future let us rather go
> In *partnership* together.

[*After Watts*]

> A golfer to his driver :

> I think of thee, I think of thee,
> And all that thou hast done for me,
> But when you fail me on the tee,
> I feel inclined to do for thee !

[*After Lewis Carroll*]

The Captain and the greenkeeper were walking o'er
    the land ;
They wept like anything to see such paucity of sand ;
"If we could dig some bunkers out," they said, "it
    would be grand."

" If forty men with forty spades delve it for half a
    year,
Do you suppose," the Captain said, " that sand
    would then appear ? "
" Maybe," replied the greenkeeper, " but 'twud be
    awfu' dear ! "

Speak gruffly to your caddy boy,
    And kick him when he sneezes ;
Your peace of mind he'll else destroy
    With grunts and groans and wheezes.

'Twas snowing, yet the wily coves
    Did play and gamble on the links :
All heated were the drying stoves,
    And loud the cry for " Drinks ! "

Beware the Pot-hunter, my son ;
    The jaws that brag, the claws that snatch ;
Beware the Spoofing Bird and shun
    The Money-maker's match.

He took his Dreadnought in his hand,
    Long time he swung as he'd been taught ;
So practised he beside the tee ;
    " I've got it now ! " he thought.

He took his Dreadnought in his hand,
Long time he swung as he'd been taught.

And as in studious thought he stood,
  The Pot-hunter, with eyes of greed,
Came strolling up in cocksure mood,
  And chuckled as he teed.

One two, one two, and straight and true
  The ball flew off with sounding smack ;
He lay stone dead, and with his " head "
  He downed the vaunted crack.

" And hast thou beat the Pot-hunter ?
  Come to my arms, my squeamish boy !
Oh, joyful day ! What ho ! What hay ! "
  He gloated in his joy.

" Will you walk a little faster ? " said the quick man
  to the slow.
" There's a hot lot just behind us, and they're asking
  ' Can't we go ? '
See how eagerly the slashers and the ' press men '
  all pursue ;
They are waiting for the signal. Will you please
  to let us through ? "

      " I'll tell you everything I can,
        There's little to relate.
      I drove into an old, old man,
        And hit him on the pate ! . . ."

'Tis the voice of the Grouser.   I heard him declare,
" You should fill up that bunker ; it's grossly un-
    fair ! "
As the ass with his footmarks, so he, with his blows,
Makes sclaffmarks and mischief wherever he goes.

When the other's in trouble, he's gay as a bird,
While fortune's on *his* side, he says not a word ;
But when the luck changes, and things don't go
    right,
He " bucks " and he curses with main and with
    might !

" You are old, Colonel Bogey," the long hitter said,
" And you putt pretty well, though you're never
    quite dead.
I always outdrive you, yet *you*'ve always won ;
Will you kindly explain how on earth it is done ? "

" Keep your head," said the sage, " don't give up ;
    never curse
When conditions are bad, for they might be much
    worse.
If your ball ' lands ' in water, sand, shingle, or gorse,
Take the rough with the smooth as ' a matter of
    course.' "

In spring, when woods are getting green,
I swear I'll play to plus eighteen.
In summer, when the days are long,
My resolution's not so strong.
In autumn, when the fields are brown,
I scan my score card with a frown.
In winter, when the fields are white,
I give up golf—except at night !

[*After Watts*]

How doth the little caddie boy
    Improve each shining club ;
He seems to find an artist's joy
    In each successful rub.

How carefully he wipes the ball,
    How neatly makes the tee,
And how I wish I could recall
    The things he says to me !

E

Local Rules

JENKINS and I were great pals at Oxford, but we have not seen much of each other since those days, and now that I am paying him a visit I feel a surprising shyness of my old friend, and an ignorance of his true character.

Jenkins has been successful in life. Patent pills have brought him riches quickly, while I, an artist, continue to grasp after fame and wealth.

I doubt whether he is really happier than I am, all the same. At all events I know that I thoroughly enjoy my rare holidays, and I am keenly looking forward to a game of golf to-morrow, though I hear that the conditions of play have altered greatly since the days when I used to spend the vacation on the east coast of Scotland.

Old "Jonks" was never very fond of exercise, I remember; and now, I am told, he has taken to golf more for the sake of appearing as a sportsman than from any real love of the grand old game.

One thing is certain : he sits up far too late to have a clear eye in the morning.

I have heard that much of the old sporting spirit of golf is dead, and that this is largely due to lenient local rules, which pander to the selfish player who thinks of his score alone.

I wonder if there is any truth in this. . . . Well, I shall know to-morrow. . . . I shall be asleep in a minute if my host does not suggest a move for bed. . . .

. . . .

There was a great crowd at the first tee.

Boys were running about and shouting "Card or pencil," "Golf card, a shilling!" And these were eagerly bought up.

Jenkins called up one of the boys.

"Will you carry for me?" he asked.

"How much?" said the boy.

"Half a crown the round."

"Not enough," said the caddie, decidedly. "I can't do it for less than five bob."

"Right!" said Jenkins.

I had read that the game was becoming expensive, but I was not quite prepared for this, and decided to carry my own clubs.

Jenkins at once strode on to the tee and drove off, ignoring the row of balls which indicated the order of precedence.

Those who were waiting did not look pleased, but as nobody objected, I also teed up.

Late hours told their tale, for both balls were badly topped and disappeared into a deep disused quarry. I descended, and carefully choosing my direction, managed to extricate myself from the bunker by playing back. Jenkins' caddie had mean-

while picked up his ball and teed it at the side of
the hazard.

My friend played, and then remarked " Two."

" I don't quite understand," I said ; " two ? "

" Yes, Local Rule," he replied. " Tee without loss.
Didn't you know ? I wondered why you played
out."

I lost that hole ; and the next.

" Let's see, what are we playing for ? " Jenkins asked ;
" shall we say pennies ? "

I had never been invited to bet on the game before, but
thinking that the loss of a few pennies could not be a
very serious matter, I agreed.

" Right," said my friend, " and the usual on the game,
of course. But as I am two up already and you don't
know the course, I'll give you one bisque."

As we proceeded on our round, things went very badly
with me.

Although I am still in my golfing teens, as regards
handicap, I felt that I could on any ordinary occasion
beat my present opponent in a fair fight. But I was
playing at a disadvantage. I evidently did not know
the rules.

Whenever Jenkins found himself in trouble, he picked
up and teed the ball without penalty, glibly quoting
" Local Rule, No. 16."

At one critical stage of the game, when Jenkins had
an easy putt for the hole, I was fortunate enough to
lay him a stymie.

" Give me my ' No Stymies '," he said to his caddie.
The latter produced a " club " furnished with teeth
which closed on the ball, and the ball was forthwith
picked up and dropped into the hole.

" Of course one would never use this club excepting
for stymies," said my opponent ; " it would not be
sporting ! "

In spite of all this, however, we were all square with
only two to play.

Now we came to a tee from which the ball had to be
lofted over some high gorse and would land out of
sight. Jenkins sent his caddie on to mark, before he
drove. The shot was a poor one and ducked quickly.

" That's in it," I remarked.

" I think not," he replied.

I hit a good one, for once, and we went forward. To
my astonishment my opponent's caddie was standing

by his ball far on the fairway, while my ball was nowhere to be seen.

We searched in vain, and finally I had to return and play another. Again I hit a good clean shot, yet this, too, joined the legion of lost balls.

Three times I played, and lost three balls.

At last, looking hard at the caddie's bulging pockets, I said, "It is curious where those balls have gone to; I'll give you this hole."

"You can't do that," said Jenkins; "you must hole out (Local Rule 510), or lose the match, and with it eighteen pounds."

"Pence," I corrected.

"Pence? What do you mean?" said Jenkins.

"We agreed to play for pennies, did we not?" I asked.

"Yes, pennies on the strokes. That is to say, if you go round in ninety-six and lose the match you pay me eight shillings, and the usual stake of a sovereign a hole as well. That is eighteen pounds, or thirty-six pounds —whichever you prefer to play."

"I think eighteen holes will be enough," I replied.

This was much more than I had bargained for. No wonder modern golf was called a rich man's game. I was too much astonished to protest, though I knew I could hardly meet my debts in the event of losing. But it was not yet too late to win, or at all events to halve the match, so returning once again I chose a very old ball, lofted it over with a mashie, and ran on to see it pitch.   The ball was not lost this time, although of course the hole was, and my opponent became dormy one.

We both reached the last green in four.

Jenkins' putt lay dead and he holed out in six.

" You've only this to halve the match," he announced, making no attempt to hide his satisfaction.

It was a long putt and a difficult one.

I had to study it for a long time before discovering the correct line to the hole.

" Looking at it won't make it any easier," my opponent remarked.

I struck the ball and found to my delight that it was travelling straight and true.

I had given it every chance and the ball rolled smoothly to the centre of the hole, rapped the back of the tin, and sat still on the edge !

"Oh, hard luck," Jenkins shouted, almost joyfully ; " that's my match.   Would you like to toss double or quits ? "

Then I remembered something.

" No, thank you," I said.   " I think we'll call it square, for I shall take a bisque ! "

.   .   .   .   .

" A biscuit ?   Certainly, old fellow ; help yourself.   I thought you were asleep.   Have another whisky and soda, too ; then I think we'll turn in.   We have a long day before us."

The Maxims of Foozler Minimus

ID facere laus est quod decet, non quod licet. "It is right to do what is decent, not only what is lawful."
Fac totum. "Hole out."
Fraus est celare fraudem. "It is illegal to waive a penalty."
Dum caput infestat, labor omnia membra molestat. "If the head moves, it upsets the machinery of all the limbs."
Aere nitent usu. "Iron clubs shine with use."

Actum ne agas. "Don't make an exhibition of yourself."
Altiora peto. "I want a higher tee."
Ante tubam trepidat. "One shivers in front of the starting-trough."
Ea sub oculis posita negligimus. "We don't keep our eyes on the ball."

40

Salus populi suprema est lex. " The safety of the public should be your first consideration."

Esse solent magno damna minora bono. " A few d——s often do a lot of good."

Audax ad omnia foemina. " A woman will go for anything."

Mens agitat molem. " Some men get annoyed with a molehill."

Corruptissima in republica plurimae leges. " Many Local Rules betray the rotten course."

Non dormit qui cus-todit. " He who plays for safety never becomes dormy."

Non omnis moriar. " Not quite dead."

Grave nihil est homini quod fert necessitas.

F

"It is not such a very serious matter for a man to be compelled to carry his own clubs."

Vestigia nulla retrorsum. "Replace the divots."

Ab uno disce omnes. "All must drive from the same disc."

Tolluntur in altum ut lapsu graviore ruant. "The higher the pitch, the deader the drop."

Fortuna non mutat genus. "Genius is not affected by fortune.

Parvum parva decent. "A short swing suits a short shot."

Firmitas in coelo. "There's safety in the sky."

Nil altum quod non placidum. "There's no pleasure in a topped ball."

Beneficia dare qui nescit injuste petit. "He who never gives a putt has no right to ask for one."

Exeunt omnes. "All out of bounds."

Wilson's Choice

I ALWAYS regarded Wilson as a bit of a crank. Since he took up golf he has become madder than ever.

When the golf wave caught up Wilson it found itself burdened with a stubborn man of mature age and a mind unbiased by traditions.

A Philp putter was to him nothing more than an unwieldy weapon peculiarly ill-adapted to its alleged purpose, and when he heard golfers reverently mention " Old Tom," he supposed that they were referring to some fine old Scottish spirit—in which surmise he was unconsciously correct.

Wilson, then, had taken up the game in a spirit of patronising boredom. After his first match he was mildly interested, after his second he was furiously angry. He had lost the match through his opponent's topped ball running through the bunker and into the hole.

Wilson went home to his study, locked the door, and for several days wrestled with the rules of golf and the various interpretations thereof.

The following Saturday, it being a wet day, he criticised these rules in detail before an unappreciative audience in the smoking-room of the Golf Club.

He gave up golf.

A week later Wilson acquired a vast expanse of un-developed land and proceeded to lay out his own course according to his own ideas.

His case against the Government was, shortly, this. That it had failed to keep pace with the American inventors. That laws framed to regulate the actions of the gutta ball had been rendered ridiculous by the un-bounded activities of irrepressible rubber. Golf, he contended, would have to be reformed.

Some said that the courses must be altered to suit the ball, others wanted a standard ball which would be made to suit the courses.

Wilson cared for neither of these proposals. He began to work out the reformation for himself.

"I have found my game at last," he wrote ; and in response to his invitation I ran down to his place for the week-end.

"Visitors take the honour," said Wilson, as we stepped on to the first tee.

I looked ahead and saw a fine expanse of flat ground with a red flag in the distance. Seeing no trouble before me, I went all out for a "joy shot," and the topped rubber scuttled quite a long way over the ground.

"This is *too* easy," I complacently remarked.

"Think so ?" said Wilson, who takes quite an in-telligent interest in politics. "Wait and see.'

He hit a good one.

As we walked forward I noticed several spaces of all

shapes and sizes enclosed in lines of tar traced out along the ground. My ball had come to rest in one of these circumscribed areas.

"Hold on," said Wilson, as I was about to play; "first let me explain the local rules. Each of these spaces represents a bunker or a hazard which may confer a favour or exact a penalty. You will observe that they are distinguished by metal discs bearing different numbers. These discs are altered by the green-keeper during the night so as to add excitement to the finding of one's fate. The numbers are explained in this book  of rules, and I may add that the rules are completely changed every month by my Secretary—a very ingenious young gentleman."

Wilson handed me a book which was in the form of a catalogue.

The number on my disc was 34. On comparing it with the same number in the book I read, "Place the ball in a bad lie and lose two strokes."

"Rather severe, isn't it?" I remarked.

" You brought it on yourself," he replied.
My opponent also found trouble from his next stroke,
however, and was disgusted to read, " Play nothing
but mixed foursomes all next week."

This upset him so much that he lost the next hole in
spite of being allowed to throw his ball on to the green
from a lucky hazard.

I had accumulated ten strokes at the next and was
still short of the green when I found a charmed circle
and was entitled to " deduct six strokes from the score."
Then I suffered a reverse.

My ball lay in 124 A, and on consulting the list I
found that I must " either kiss the caddie or concede
the hole." After one horrified glance at the gardener's
boy I put the ball in my pocket.

Bad luck cost me the next hole also, for I lay on a
small patch of the green marked 3¾ and read, " Dead
stymie ; putt with a niblick."

Shortly after this my host sliced into a little spot some
way off the course and was compelled to pay me a
sovereign, but I soon lost this advantage by pulling
into 142 C, which decreed that I should stand my
host a dinner at the Ritz.

I need not pursue the game through the changes and
chances of this exciting round. The luck was fairly
evenly distributed, I recollect.

My opponent had to play a certain hole with one hand
and on one foot, while I had to putt on my knees with
my eyes shut.

On another occasion he was allowed three free kicks, after which I could take a penalty hit at his ball.

Other places which I visited condemned me to play ten strokes with a gutta ball, buy a club from the local professional, and invent a new golf story, while my host suffered the painful punishment of having to laugh at my golf story, play for five minutes with bare feet, and watch his caddie play one hole while he carried the clubs.

" Well, what do you think of it ? " Wilson inquired, as we finished the round.

" It is not golf," I replied, " but I'm not sure that it is not more entertaining than the modern game of chance which is supplanting the royal and ancient trial of strength and skill."

The "Lonesome"

"TALKING of left-handed golfers," said the Doctor, who never scruples to adulterate fact with fiction in his effort to sustain the interest of his tales, "I know a young fellow who was trained from infancy to play golf ambidextrously. He could wield a club equally well either right- or left-handed. This, of course, necessitated his employing two caddies, with a double set of clubs. Nor was that all. Sometimes he would play right-handed back-handed, and at other times back-handed left-handed, if you follow me."

"That must have been very confusing to his opponents," I remarked.

"His opponents?" the story-teller repeated thoughtfully. "Ah, now, that's the funny part about it. He never had any! Nobody would play with him, you see, on account of his peculiarities. He entered for all the Club competitions, however, and the Committee were compelled to rate him at three separate handicaps. Under one he was permitted to play right-handed, under another left-handed, and under the third he was at liberty to address himself to each stroke in any manner that he pleased.

"It is a noteworthy fact that, whereas he was scratch in the first place, and plus two in the second, his allowance when he had the choice of playing either way was minus eight. This caused him great vexation, for it prevented him from attaining the height of his ambition, namely, to enter for the Amateur Championship. At the same time it probably saved the Championship management from a very perplexing dilemma, for they would, of course, have been compelled to draw him against three different opponents, giving him, in consequence, three chances to one against all other competitors.

"The difference in his handicaps must, I think, be put down to the fact that he never could decide in what manner he might make use of his extraordinary talents to the best advantage. He would address the ball first with one club, then he would turn round and see how it felt the other way with another club, until by constant grounding he appreciably improved the lie. People naturally objected to this, with the result that his thoughts were distracted, and however good the resultant shot might be, he was always disturbed by the doubt whether he might not have succeeded even better had he adopted the other method.

"A sad story, is it not? It all goes to show how disadvantageous it may be to overburden oneself with the good things of our golfing world.

"Well, as I was telling you, he was reduced to playing against himself, right hand versus left, and I daresay he would have enjoyed his matches well enough, had it not been for one unfortunate failing. He was a very

G

bad loser ! He couldn't *bear* to be beaten, and for a long time he arranged matters so cleverly that he halved all his matches on the last green. Now comes the tragedy.

" I happened to be passing the eighteenth green one day last week, when I noticed my poor young friend grovelling on the ground in evident distress. I was about to offer my professional assistance when I discovered the cause of his excitement. His right-hand game had been laid a dead stymie by its opponent.

" It was quite an easy putt, but he obstinately refused to accept the expert advice that I offered him, with the inevitable result that his right hand lost the match.

" The disgrace was unbearable. Just think of it. He had been beaten by himself ! "

The Doctor rose to go.

" I should very much like to meet this remarkable player," I scoffed ; " is he a member of your club ? "

" He *was*," the Doctor gravely replied ; " but now he is gone, poor fellow, gone to his long rest."

" Dead ? " I callously inquired.

" Oh, no," the Doctor cried in seemly horror ; " he has been admitted to the Home for Unendurables, of which I have the honour to be a visiting physician."

From Tee to Tee

"I MAY AS WELL WARN YOU that I've got my driving back."

"Well, I've got a tennis elbow, so we'll be about quits."

"How DO I STAND, CADDIE?" inquired an old duffer who had been putting very poorly. "You've this for an improbable 'alf, sir," was the reply.

A NOTORIOUSLY CLOSE-FISTED MAN was taking his golfing holiday in Scotland and had, by hard bargaining, managed to secure the exclusive services of a first class caddie who was known to be a very good player. "Mind, now," said the ambitious Southerner, "I expect to receive some really good tips from you during my stay here, you understand." "Aye," replied the Scotsman, hitching up the heavy bag, "an' ah'm expectin' the like frae ye, ye ken."

"I LIKE TO PLAY with Captain Hart,"
    Miss Grabb was heard to say;
"He has such strength, combined with art,
    And such a ' winning way.'"

"DO YOU DRIVE OFF YOUR RIGHT LEG ?"
"I really couldn't tell you, but I jolly nearly sliced off one of my left toes this morning !"

English Visitor: "I did the next hole in one last time I was here."
Scotch Caddie (unmoved): "Ah, weel, ye'll likely tak' six to it to-day."

FROM A FRENCH COURSE :
"What's the French for 'match play' ?"
"Why, 'jeu des allumettes,' of course."

PLEASANT PROSPECT FOR JONES, who has started on a golfing holiday with a bad-tempered foozler :
The B.F. (on the third green) : "If I lose another hole I shall go straight home !"

A SHORT HANDICAP PLAYER had arrived at a fashionable resort on the French coast just in time to compete for a coveted medal. Most of the members had already fixed up their matches, and he was compelled to play with a French gentleman who was quite a beginner and ignorant of the rules. The visitor started well, but

was slightly bothered by his companion's persistent
attempts at conversation, since his own knowledge of the
language only ran to such phrases as "Bien joué," "Pas
de chance," etc.   He had a fine score, however, with
only two holes to play, when a storm of rain suddenly
burst upon them and the Frenchman made straight for
the club-house.   He protested and gesticulated wildly
when the other tried to detain him, and at last broke
away.   "Oh, why," groaned the Englishman, left
without a partner, "was I never taught the French for
'You are not allowed to take shelter during a stroke
competition'?"

FROM A DAILY PAPER'S REPORT of alterations to a Golf
Club-house :
"The builders have been busy with additions to the
club-house. . . . The old ladies' room has been taken
for a smoking-room."

" CADDIE, SIR ? "

" Yes, but I want a boy who can count, for I'm playing for the medal to-day. Can you add up, my boy ? "

" Yessir."

" Well, what's five and seven and four ? "

" Twelve, sir."

" Come along ; you'll do."

" WHEN I'M REALLY OFF MY GAME," said Riley, who had not made a decent shot all day, " I can play as badly as the best of them ! "

Crabbie (after a duffed drive at the sixth) : " How often have I told you not to stand where I can see you while I'm driving, boy ? " *Caddie* (after some calculations) : " Six, sir."

Excited Spinster (waving a score card) : " Congratulate me, Captain ; I'm seventy-seven to-day." *Captain Gallant :* " No, really ? By Jove, you don't look it."

A GOLFER, who was taking part in a foursome on a strange course, questioned his caddie as to the capabilities of his opponents as the party left the first tee.

"Well, sir," said the youth, "that tall gent takes some beating. He plays with his head." "And the other?" asked the visitor. "Ah, he wants some watching, sir," said the caddie, "for *he* plays with his *feet!*"

"WHAT ARE THE HAZARDS on your home course?" someone asked a pro. who was competing in an open meeting.

"Mostly trees, sir," was the reply.

"Does it provide a good test of golf?" asked the other.

"It certainly demands play of a very high order," said the diplomatically truthful player.

The Colonel (to a mild man who has driven into him) : "How dare you play, sir, before I am out of range?"

Mild man : "But didn't I see you wave us on?"

The Colonel : "Certainly not: I was waving you *off!*"

FROM A BOOK OF CHILDREN'S VERSES :

"Your ball bounces high !
Do you ever think why ?
There's a fairy inside it without any doubt ;
A poor prisoned fairy who wants to get out."

Sheila Braine.

A GOLFER'S ADDITION :

"In the case of a golf ball—a case that is thin—
There's a poor devil putting who wants to get *in!*"

"DID YOU HAVE A GOOD GAME?" a beginner was asked after his first match.

"Grand," he replied. "He won ten and nine, I won the bye five and four, he won the by-bye three and one, and I won the last hole—so we halved the match, you see."

"WHEN I WAS OUT IN THE WEST," said the globe-trotter, "I was invited to play in a match between two  clubs which were bitter rivals. My opponent was a huge, fierce-looking cowboy, who drove with tremendous force, but I soon established a lead by running down some exceptionally long putts. The ninth hole was situated in a very wild and lonely spot, and here my opponent, speaking for the first time, drawled 'Say, stranger, I reckon you're putting well.' 'Yes,' I said complacently, 'I'm not doing so badly.' 'Say, stranger,' he continued, producing a murderous-looking knife, and fixing me with his eye, 'I reckon you're putting a darn sight *too* well!' And do you know I wasn't nearly so successful with my putts going home."

" Is there Sunday play in this Club," inquired
the smart young man who had arrived by motor from
London. " Yes, sir," said the steward ; "Sunday
play with caddies over eighteen." " But I don't want
to play with a bally caddie," said the visitor, " especially if his handicap is over eighteen ! "

A short-sighted old golfer who after six very
strenuous shots had
at last succeeded in
dislodging his ball
from a heavy lie, was
seen to be searching
anxiously along the
ground. " I've found
most of the divots,
sir," cried the caddie,
running back with
several large lumps of
turf. " Divots be

d——d ! " cried the infuriated foozler ; "it's my *false
teeth* I'm looking for."

A dance had been arranged by the members of a golf
club in Egypt, and the genial Scottish secretary was
acting as master of the ceremonies. It was a Saturday,
and at midnight, when the fun was at its height, the
secretary, acting on the suggestion of one of the older
members, announced that the dancing would cease.

H

There was a cry of disappointment, and the guests reluctantly prepared to depart. Suddenly the cannie Scot, who had left the ballroom for a moment, returned with a copy of "Whitaker" in his hand. "Ladies and gentlemen," he said, "I think we can keep it up a little longer, for I find that it will not be Sunday for nearly three hours yet *in Scotland !*"

"Is THIS A BAD COURSE for losing one's balls ? "
"Yes, but it's a splendid one for finding other people's ! "

A CLERGYMAN was travelling in a railway carriage with a team of golfers who were celebrating their victory by circulating the whisky-flask. "Do you know, sir," said the conscientious parson, "that I have never tasted a drop of whisky in all my life ?" "Naw," said the bottle-holder, entirely mistaking his intentions, "and ye're no goin' to begin now, neither ! "

HELPFUL HINT for golfing motorists :
"An unbreakable neck for drivers has just been patented."

First novice (watching a professional in difficulties) :
" Why did he throw the ball over his left shoulder ?"
Second novice : " Oh, just for luck."

THE FOOZLER's now frightened clean out of his wits
  At the fate of his favourite shots :
Oh, pity poor parties who potter in pits
  On those courses all pitted with pots !

"WHAT *am* I doing ? " roared the Hibernian "late
beginner " as he foozled his sixteenth successive tee
shot. "'Itting the ball on the top," drawled the dis-
interested caddie. "Why didn't you tell me that
before ? " demanded the sufferer. "Tee the d——d
thing *upside down*."

A GOLFER who had a peculiarly energetic style was
anxious to call forth some encouraging remark from
his taciturn caddie. "Don't you think I'm playing
better to-day ? " he asked. "Mebbe ye'd no do so
bad," was the reply, " if ye wud'na rin after the baa'
afore ye've hit it ! "

THE SHORT-SIGHTED FOOZLER stood watching from a
distance while one of the groundsmen raked through
a big bunker. "Thank goodness," he murmured, as
he turned away, "there's someone who plays nearly
as badly as I do ! "

A FRENCHMAN, visiting England for the first time, was
taken to see a game of golf. "What do you think of
it ? " his host inquired, after showing him round.
"Magnifique ! " cried the foreigner, " bot I think eet

ees vair difficult."   "I'm glad you realise that," said the other.   "Those who have never played the game seldom appreciate its difficulties."   "Ah, bot I think eet shall be *vair* difficult," the Frenchman repeated, "to balance ze ball on zat so little heap of sand!"

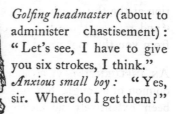

Golfing headmaster (about to administer chastisement): "Let's see, I have to give you six strokes, I think." *Anxious small boy*: "Yes, sir. Where do I get them?"

YOUNG SLASHER, who considered that his style was an improvement on that of Harry Vardon, had persuaded a friend to snap him in the act of driving. "I think," said he, "that ought to turn out a perfect model of the ideal golfing swing, don't you?" "The answer," replied the photographer, "is in the negative."

FROM A CITY SCHOOL OF GOLF:
Fashionable Lady: "What?   Grip the stick with both hands?   And how, pray, am I to hold up my skirt?"

Foozler Minor: "Par for this course is sixty-seven." *Foozler Minimus*: "Is he, by Jove? . . . What's Mar?"

ON THE FIRST GREEN.
Tennis Player (keen on golf) : " What's the score ? "
Golfer (keen on tennis) : " Fifteen all ! "

" DO YOU RECOVER GOLF BALLS ? " said the beginner, rushing into the professional's shop. " Yes, sir," the assistant replied. " Then just run over to the plantation at the thirteenth hole," cried the agitated novice, " and recover those half-dozen balls which I bought from you this morning ! "

AN INFLUENTIAL VISITOR was being pressed for his opinion of a rough, but not ready, course which had been extensively advertised. " I can truthfully say this," said the stranger, who had lost four balls during the round, " it provides a very searching test."

" THE PROFESSOR is the most absent-minded man that I know. After cleaning his ball with the contents of his tobacco pouch, he took out his ball-cleaner and tried to fill his pipe with the sponge ! "

A VERY MODEST FOREIGNER who was learning golf had been persuaded to play a match with a long handicap man. " Have you tell him that I play very bad ? " he inquired of the secretary, who had fixed up the game. " Yes, I told him that you were quite a beginner," the latter replied. " Then please to tell him," said the modest man, " that I am even worse than he thinks I am ! "

"WHAT'S THE DIFFERENCE between a professional and an amateur?" "One plays for pay, and the other pays for play!"

AN OLD LADY was proudly displaying a cup which had been won by her niece and nephew in a mixed foursome competition. "Very handsome," said the visitor, "and I see that it is inscribed 'Vi et Arte.' What does that mean?" The old lady put on her spectacles. "Ah, that is the names," she said, "Violet and Arthur, you know!"

McFOOTLE was partnering his son in a foursome which the boy was very keen to win. The old man, unfortunately, began by slicing very badly, and at last exclaimed: "A' canna play straight the day, Jock, what will a' dae?" To which his son earnestly replied, "Pu', Pa, *pu*'! Can ye no *pu*', Pa?"

FOOZLER MAXIMUS, having missed the ball six times in succession, suddenly turned to his tiny caddie and fiercely demanded, "What am I doing, and why?"

"I PLAYED off my tie this morning." "That's nothing; I played off three of my waistcoat buttons!"

"WINDY?" repeated the Yankee, who was playing in a gale. "Guess you've never experienced a tornado? Why, I know a course where the trouble is to keep the ball *down*. I lost a ball once when

putting on the last green. It was caught up into the air and I never saw it again, and that ball, sir, was weighted with two ounces of lead. Windy? I reckon this is a mere cat's-paw."

BOOKS FOR GOLFERS :
"The Best Holes and How to Make Them," by P. Rabbit. (Burroughs, Green & Co.) "How *Not* to Play," by Those Who Know. (Foozler Bros.) "Theory is Better than Practice," by Freake Putter.

" How to Get Down to Scratch," by Dogge-Legge. Block on " The Green." (Swears & Growler.) " It Never Could Happen Again," by Fluker. (Clubb, Bore & Son.) " Why Taylor Can't Beat Me," by the Author of " Why I Don't Want to Beat Taylor." (Dead Trumpeter Ltd.) " The Vale of Tares," by the Author of " Golf Faults Advocated." (Longwind, Proser & Co.)

" DID YOU WIN, Colonel ? " " No, I lost." " Badly ? " " Certainly not. I'm a very *good* loser ! "

Busybody (accosting a professional at the crisis of an important money match) : " Can you tell me whether you played your approach to the thirteenth hole at

Sloggington on April 14, 1893, with a mid-iron or a driving mashie ? "

THE SLASHER had driven far out of bounds, and a boy came quickly back waving a ball in the air. " This is not the one I lost," said the wild driver, examining an old gutty. "No, sir," said the thoughtless youth, "but then, you see, it's not the one I picked up."

FROM THE MIXED FOURSOMES :
Gushing Young Lady (to bashful youth who has won their match by a long putt on the last green): "Oh, *pretty* partner !"

A SCOTSMAN was visiting a London course. "How many have you played?" his opponent asked, when they had reached the first green. "'E's played eight," said the Scotsman's caddie. "You should say '*we* have played eight,'" his employer told him; "the caddie is regarded as part of the match. You and I are partners, you see, and you must do all you can to assist me, since our interests are the same." The visitor soon found his game, and won two-and-sixpence on the match and on the bye. "Who won?" asked a member, as they left the last green. "*We* won, sir," said the caddie; "half-a-crown each !"

"How DO YOU STAND, Tippler?" "He's dymie— I mean stormy—that is——" (Left in trouble.)

THE KINDLY CADDIE-MASTER, who was officiating at the caddies' annual treat, asked a small boy with a big appetite, "Will ye tak' anither bannock, Archie?" "Naw," said the boy. "Naw—what?" the caddie-master suggested. "Naw, *dammit*," cried the youngster, "are ye deaf?"

Golfer (explaining the game to a foreigner): "They are now waiting to see who is furthest away from the hole. Each wants the other to putt first."
Foreigner: "Zat is vat you call ze Etiquette of Golf, yes?"

Duffer (who has driven the ball of his life): "I don't want *that* back."
Disagreeable Man: "I do, though. You were in front of the tee!"

A GOLFER who had been making a long stay at a winter health resort tipped his old caddie as he was leaving and said, "Good-bye, John, I hope you will carry for me again next year." "Ah, sir," said the old fellow, dolefully, "anything may 'appen before that." "Oh, come," cried the visitor, "I shall expect to see you here for many years yet." "Them's the very words as was said by the gent I carried for last winter," the caddie replied, "and a fortnight afterwards I 'eard as 'e was dead!"

A SHORT-TEMPERED PLAYER, who had loudly ejaculated "Damn" on missing his first drive, turned round to find a parson standing close beside the tee. "I must apologise for my language," he said. "I accept your apology," the parson replied, "for the shot was really not worth a ' Damn ' ! "

Stranger (looking for the links) : "Have you heard of any golf being played in these parts? "
Yokel : "Naw, but I be rather 'ard of 'earing."

FROM THE ADVERTISEMENT OF A CONTINENTAL HOTEL :
"Eighteen-hole golf course, which has just been constructed in ten minutes."
Another record.

You may break, you may shatter your clubs, if you will,
But the cause of your foozles will stick to you still.

A STUDIOUS MIDDLE-AGED PARSON had taken up golf under the tuition of a young enthusiast. For months he foozled every stroke, but at last he hit a " hummer " nearly three hundred yards down the fairway, and his young teacher excitedly awaited an outburst of joy. The late beginner slowly picked up his bag. "Have you read Boswell's 'Life of Johnson'?" he inquired.

Rude Little Urchin (to tremendously swell youth, who is carrying his clubs down Piccadilly): "'Ere, *come on*, boy; can't yer see I want a mashie?"

THE OVER-ZEALOUS NEW SECRETARY, suddenly looking up from his work, saw two keen old duffers who were finishing an exciting match. Each putted three times, but neither succeeded in holing out. Mindful of his instructions, the Secretary threw open the window and called out, "Gentlemen, *please!* It is strictly forbidden to practise putting on the home green!"

THERE WAS A LARGE CROWD on the first tee waiting to start for the Bank Holiday sweepstake, and everyone was silently praying that Major Savage, the slowest player and worst-tempered member of the Club, would get well away. There was dead silence as the Major finished a perfect trial swing; then a short-sighted young foozler rushed forward and exclaimed, " Fine shot, sir. That's the longest ball I've ever seen you hit ! "

FROM THE CHILDREN'S COURSE :
" Come on."
" Wait a bit. I've lost myself ! "

> NO LONGER on our course we blaze
> In staring scarlet coats,
> Since to the sheep put out to graze
> They've added bull and goats.

> Our cup of sorrow now is full ;
> We're " bos "-eyed, one and all ;
> With one eye fixed upon the bull,
> The other on the ball !

A VISITOR who had been boasting of the great distances which he was accustomed to cover with his tee shots had foozled the first five drives. " My short game seems to be better than my long game to-day," he remarked, as he fluked a run-up into the hole. " It is certainly *longer*," said his candid companion.

Lady Secretary (to novice from a suburban course) : " What's your par ! "
Novice : " Pork butcher. What's yours ? "

"I HEAR that you spent your holiday in the Engadine, Captain Keene. Tell me which peak impressed you most of all those noble masses of eternal snow?" "Well, I forget its name, but it's that one which gives the line to the fourth hole."

A VERY NERVOUS PLAYER, who had occasion to drop a ball, was suddenly seen to writhe and wriggle his body, jump up and down, and clutch at the small of his back. "Whatever is the matter?" cried his partner, hastening up. "Confound it all!" gasped the contortionist. "I've dropped the beastly thing down the back of my neck!"

WHO MINDS his muscles and neglects his brains,
Will lose in bunkers what in length he gains.
The wise man ponders, ere he strikes a blow,
How, why, and where he wants the ball to go.

A NERVOUS GOLFER, while travelling for his health's sake, played a game against a burly "squatter" far up

country in Australia. The "new chum's" skill pre-
vailed against the stronger man's muscle, and the
former held a commanding lead at the turn. On
coming to a very lonely and desolate part of the course,
the Australian grounded his club in a bunker. "Here,
you can't do that," said the visitor. "How do you
know?" the player inquired. "It's forbidden," was
the reply; "I can prove it to you, if you like, for I've
got the St. Andrews Rules in my pocket." "Ah,
but I've got the *Local* Rules in mine," said his adver-
sary, as he whipped out
a revolver.

"TAYLOR in the morning
reached the turn one
stroke before anybody
else," says a report.

THERE are three classes
of people who are entitled to refer to themselves as
"We." They are Kings, Editors, and Caddies.

Visitor (on new course) : "Are you going to invite the
professionals to open the links?"
Secretary (busy replacing divots) : "No, I fancy that
the members can manage that for themselves!"

"EXCUSE ME, sir," said the Club "Buttons" to a thirsty
visitor, "are you a member of this Club?" "Why?"

asked the stranger. "'Cos if you're not, sir," said the boy, "I'm not allowed to serve you with any *excitable* drinks!"

FROM AN OLD COMPLAINT BOOK :

> Some dashing young golfers, I see,
> Wear trousers which end at the knee.
> 'Twere better by half
> Just to cover the calf—
> At least, where the calf ought to be!

A LONG-HANDICAP MAN who had been expectantly watching a young golfer calmly slashing off daisy heads with unerring accuracy was astonished to see him subsequently top his drive into the nearest bunker.

"Seems to be rather a 'lackadaisycal' player," he remarked.

ANDREW KIRKALDY once topped his ball into the Swilcan when going to the first hole. A spectator, out for some cheap instruction, asked, "How did you manage to miss that one?" "A' never hit the d——d thing," was the reply.

"WHAT's the distance here, caddie?"
"About *one hit*."

ONE OFTEN WONDERS whether professionals are subject
to fits of "nerves" with the worst of us. When the
question was put to the most modest of champions he
replied, "I can remember one such occasion. While
playing in a very important match I was greatly
worried by a spectator—a lady, I regret to say—who
kept close to me and talked in a high-pitched tone to
her companion during the stroke. At last I could
stand it no longer. I stopped in the act of addressing
the ball, turned round, and looked at her. She proceeded to finish her sentence, then nodded towards me
and said, 'All right. You
can go on now. *I've
finished.*' "

Ferocious Player (who has
grounded his club in a
doubtful hazard): "Is
this a bunker?"
Timid Opponent: "Er—
not if you don't want it
to be!"

"I'M getting on fine with my golf, Father: the pro.
gave me three strokes this morning and we finished all
square."
"That's good, my boy: where did you take your
strokes?"
"Why, at every hole, of course."

K

"Is this a long hole?" inquired the visitor, as he peered over the edge of a Downland "Hades." "About four hundred yards," said his partner, "as the mole burrows."

From the secretary's post-bag :
" Dear Sir,

I should feel very greatfull if you would kindly speak to a lad named Smith, he is and has been quite a terror to my Son.   He is calling him big head fat head and all kind of Names and throwing at him and of course last evening he done the same in return my Son called him back were upon he started fighting him, you can see the eye he has got and with what voilence he must have hit for a great fellow like him to use a boy like that is disgraseful we are a great mind to take a summonds out but we trust to your kindness perhaps if you will speak to him it might stop further trububle,
yrs. etc. ———."

At a committee meeting :
The grandfather of the Club.   "Gentlemen, there's a *thistle* growing on the new sixteenth ! "

From Ireland :
" Whose honour ! "
" *Your* honour, your honour."

'THERE was a fellow playing in front of me this morning," said the slasher, " who evidently didn't know the etiquette of the game. I drove into him at the thirteenth, and the beggar didn't even wait for me to come up and apologise."

THE BEST COURSES are nearly always difficult of access. In order to reach a certain well-known course it is necessary to wait for nearly half an hour at a small junction which is only two miles distant from the links. An irritable golfer who was stamping up and down the platform one cold morning was heard to exclaim, " I've been a member of —— for thirty years, and during that time I reckon I've spent eight months at this d——d station."

Infuriated Farmer (to golfer who has driven out of bounds and is vigorously searching for his ball among the growing crops) : " Now then, you've no business to be there ! "
Golfer : " I know.   Rotten shot, wasn't it ? "

DURING A BOGEY COMPETITION :
" What are you down in ? "
" Twelve ; *but I get a stroke !* "

SYMPATHY is wasted on some people. A well-known amateur had driven a long but erratic ball at a critical stage of the game. "I'm afraid you're in the bunker," said his opponent; "I'm sorry."
"Sorry be blowed," cried the other; "I only hope *you*'ll be in it too!"

"THERE is a very interesting new decision by the Rules Committee entitled 'Error in Bogey Card.'"
"Ah, I'm glad they've caught the old gentleman tripping at last."

> SOME men, their loss to sweeten,
>   Will never own defeat:
> While others, if they're beaten,
>   Don't know when they are beat!

Foozler Minimus (to a couple of French ladies who have suddenly appeared in front): "Avez-vous coupé dans?"

> WHEN Colonel Damm went off at golf
>   His language, sad to say,
> So shocked his wife that *she* went off;
>   In fact, she ran away.

> The wicked Colonel cried "Hurrah!"
>   And sailed for sunny seas;
> Now in Ceylon—most singular—
>   He swears by single-ease.

THE FOOZLER had hit a good shot, for once. The caddie dropped the bag and loudly clapped his hands. "Thank you, my boy," said the old gentleman, "I think that stroke really did deserve some applause."

"A' was na' applaudin'," the caddie replied, "A' was just scarin' them *craws* frae the green!"

"YOU MUST REMEMBER, SIR," said the professional from Ireland, "that when you are looking down on

the ball you can see only two-thirds of it. The other two-thirds is out of sight, and that's the part you must aim at!"

ON A CROWDED HOLIDAY COURSE a novice had apparently lost his ball, and the couple behind, after waiting some time, requested to be allowed to pass. "Why?" demanded the obstructor. "You have lost your ball, haven't you?" said the other. "Certainly not," replied the slow player, consulting his watch, "I shall not have lost it for nearly three minutes yet!"

" WHAT's the charge for visitors at this club ? "
" Half a crown a day, sir."
" Well, I have to return to Town this afternoon. Give me *a shilling's* worth, will you ? "

GARDEN-PARTY GOLF :
" What have I got to do ? "
" Tee yourself up, hit yourself through that hoop, and hole yourself out ! "

TWO VERY WAYWARD ONES were enraged at being driven into. "Sorry," said the man behind ; "I didn't know you belonged to this hole ! "

Col. Chalk (to Sclaffer, who is about to attempt a long screw back) : " Mind you don't cut my cloth."

Sclaffer (serenely) : " All right, old chap, don't worry ; I'll replace the divot ! "

A GOLFER who was visiting a municipal course without having previously fixed up a match had picked up an opponent who was favoured by remarkable luck during the first few holes. " This is evidently your day out," he remarked. "Only 'arf a day," was the reply. "I must be back by six to lay the cloth for dinner."

ONE of the applicants for the post of golf club secretary put forward as his chief recommendation that he had had previous experience as secretary to a gas company.

THE SECRETARY had found the stranger a match. "I think it only fair to warn you that he's a parson," he said. "Why?" the stranger asked.
"Because otherwise," said the secretary, "you might never have known it."

Novice (after watching two rounds of professional play): "I suppose this is what you call 'clock golf'?"

"Do you get many week-enders here, boy?"
"Yessir, but most of the players are weak all round!"

A PROFESSIONAL PHOTOGRAPHER had planted his apparatus in front of the first teeing-ground during the opening of a new course, and had appealed to the spectators to keep still and silent.
Voice from the front row: "Anybody can have my place for a sovereign!"

"WHICH is the way to the golf links, Tommy?" said a golfer to a small boy whom he met on the road. "How

do you know my name's Tommy ?" the boy asked.
"Oh, I just guessed," the visitor replied. "Then
you can just guess the way to the golf," said the youth
as he walked on.

AN IMPETUOUS PLAYER, annoyed at being kept back
by a couple of duffers, drove off at a blind hole before
they were out of range.
"I think I have given them a good start," he
remarked. "I should think you must have, sir," his
caddie replied.

> WHEN you find the bunker, mind you
>   Fill the holes wherein you stand.
> Don't depart and leave behind you
>   Footprints in the silver sand.
>
> Footprints which unless you smother,
>   By some other may be found ;
> He'll say something worse than " Bother ! "
>   If you spoil his medal round.

" THE POOR OLD PROFESSOR is becoming more absent-
minded every day," said the secretary, looking out of
the smoking-room window. "He has just stuck his
putter into the hole and is walking in with the flag-
post sticking out of his bag ! "

AN IMPETUOUS PLAYER, who was following behind two
stout old duffers, sent his caddie forward at a blind hole,

and was very impatient of the constant reply, "Not yet, sir," to his insistent demand "Is it safe?" "You can go now, sir," the boy sang out at last. "They've both of 'em gone down a rabbit 'ole!"

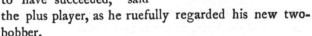

"SORRY, partner," said Basher, after badly topping his approach, "I was trying to put a lot of cut on the ball." "You seem to have succeeded," said the plus player, as he ruefully regarded his new two-bobber.

THE IRRITABLE BEGINNER, who had been asking advice of his caddie all the way round, finally completely lost his temper through missing a short putt on the last green, and flung his club among some members who were having tea on the Club house lawn. "What did I do *then?*" he inquired of the boy who went to fetch the club. "Made a d——d fool of yourself, sir," was the candid reply.

SAID the duffer, "Now, boy, for the bye,"
And the caddie replied, with a sigh,
  "If you can't win the bye,
  By-the-bye, you might try
The *by*-by-by-bye, by and by."

L

" How do you like our course ? " the secretary in-quired of a visitor from France. " Ah, *awfully plus !* " was the gushing reply.

FROM A CLUB NOTICE BOARD :
" If the GENTLEMAN (?) who removed three new balls from Mr. Jones' great-coat pocket *by mistake* will return the same to their rightful owner he will hear of something to his advantage."

" MANY ' FLANNELLED FOOLS ' in the north-eastern part of Scotland have made names for themselves on the golf links," a daily paper tells us. They were probably afraid that names might otherwise be made for them by Mr. Rud-yard Kipling.

Boy on the road (to an old gentleman who has been anxiously searching for his ball for nearly five min-utes) : " Go it, Field-Marshal, you're getting 'ot ! "

A BRAWNY " TYKE," who was having his first lesson in golf, started to let out at the ball with all his might, and seemed thoroughly to enjoy the exercise in spite of the fact that he failed to shift the ball any great distance. " Easy, sir ; you're pressing," cried the horrified professional. " Slow back ; don't try to do too much at first." " See here, young mon," said his pupil, dropping his club, " if A' can no hit as hard as A' can, where's t' fun in t' game ? "

First Novice : "What do you call those competitions where you keep each other's cards and count the strokes ? "
Second Novice : " A *medal-some*, I believe."

A LITTLE GIRL, who had been taken to see a game of golf for the first time in her life, happened to arrive at the finish of a match which depended on the putting on the last green. The players were down on their knees, silently scanning the line to the hole. " Oh, Mamma," cried the child, " look at those men all saying their prayers ! "

> HE that at the game would thrive
> Must learn to putt as well as drive.

Visitor (uncertain whether it is safe to drive off) : " Can I hit them, boy ? "
Caddie (disgusted at having to wait behind the slowest couple on the course) : " Yes, if you like, sir ! "

THE BEGINNER, whose score when shorn of a long handicap proved to be ten under bogey, stood ready to receive the prize. "How did you manage it?" somebody asked. "I was lucky all through," replied the novice, "for I started with an old gutty, and when I looked at my ball on the last green I found I was playing with a rubber-core nearly new."

FROM A NOVEL:
"The head waiter, a tall and gentlemanly person with the manners of a golf club secretary, gave personal  attention to their insistent needs." It must be very comforting to a man who is temporarily out of a job in the one profession to know that he is perfectly qualified to fulfil the duties of the other.

Visitor (approaching plateau green): "What's this, caddie? A quarter mashie?"
Caddie: "No, sir; *a full putter.*"

First Novice: "What is a 'rub of the green'?"
Second Novice: "I'm not quite sure, but I know it has been prohibited by the new rules."

Parson (to opponent whose language is a wee bit free) :
" I must really request you, sir, to have some respect
for the cloth."
Stranger : " Why, —— it all, we're not playing
billiards ! "

" I've just finished a most exciting match," shouted
an old Dottievillian. " I played me against myself.
One of me was dormy one, and we lay as we liked on
the last green, but then I went and stymied myself, so
that both of us ended the round all square."

Topping (reckoning the odds in a foursome) : " They
get eight and four, and we get twelve and five ; what's
the difference ? "
Grabbet : " Three and ninepence—in our favour."

From France :
Jones (arriving at the links) : " Er—combien, cocher ? "
" *Cocher* " (late of Fulham) : " Frank and a 'arf,
guv'nor."

The Dean, who was drawn to play with the Colonel
in a foursome competition, knew that the only chance
of victory lay in keeping his partner in a good temper.
The parson was short-sighted, but, seeing the Colonel
take a tremendous whack at the ball, he called out,
" Well done, sir. Good shot. Thank you, that's
just where I wanted to be."   Then, turning anxiously

to his caddie, he whispered, "Where is it, my boy?"
"He's missed it altogether," was the discomfiting
reply.

First-class Caddie (reading the paper): "What's these
'ere 'domes of silence,' Jack?"
Second-class Caddie: "I reckon maybe they're what
the Colonel says when 'e tops 'is drive in a mixed
foursome."

FROM THE LADIES' LINKS, during the one club com-
petition:
Unattractive Novice (about to approach a bunker):
"Oh, I do wish I had a *masher*."

"SANDY hit a spectator in the Championship
yesterday."
"No doubt he fully deserved it!"

THE PROFESSOR, who was delighted at having holed a
long putt for the match on the last green, modestly
awaited the congratulations of his opponent, a young
'Varsity "man." The silence was at last broken
by the youth's impetuous outburst, "How simply
sickening!"

Officious Stranger: "You get some wonderful views
on this course, don't you?"
Secretary: "Wonderful. Especially from the visitors."

Muddlehead: "Do you use the over-grappling lip? I mean the over-lipping grap—that is, the——" (Left bunkered.)

A SELF-SATISFIED LONDONER was paying his first visit to a famous Scottish green and, happening to be off his game, gave vent to some very strong language. At last he turned fiercely on his old caddie and demanded, "Do *you* know what I am doing?" "Aye," said the Scot. "A' ken fine what ye're daein'—but Ah'm no' sae blaspheemious as tae say!"

FOOZLER MINIMUS had been taken to see an Exhibition match, but he seemed to take little interest in the proceedings, and his uncle, who had eagerly watched each stroke, had almost forgotten the boy's presence by the time they reached the last green. Here one of the Triumvirate, who was left with a putt for the match, having walked up and down for some minutes in order to view the line from every aspect, finally 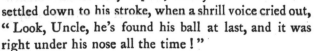 settled down to his stroke, when a shrill voice cried out, "Look, Uncle, he's found his ball at last, and it was right under his nose all the time!"

HIS OPPONENT'S CADDIE having moved while the Colonel was putting, the latter turned round and boxed the boy's ears. " My hole," his opponent announced ; "you hit my caddie."

"DID YOU BEAT YOUR MAN this morning ?" a golfer inquired of a novice who had been playing on a Municipal course. "Oh, he's not *my* man," was the reply, " he's the head waiter at the Grand Hotel."

MODERN GOLF COURSES are often constructed mainly for the purpose of increasing the value of prospective building land. A famous pro. had been invited to plan out eighteen holes in connection with a new estate. " Ye'll just tee up here," he said, after carefully considering the lie of the land, "and start to play over yon meadow." "We can't do that," said the agent, "for it is intended to put up villas all along here." "Aweel, it's a pity," said the designer, "but we'll just hae to take this ither direction an'——." "We can't go that way either," said his companion, "for that's where the big Hotel will be erected, and beyond that again we are going to construct——" "Luk here," the pro. interrupted, "ah'm thinkin' maybe we'd better gang a wee bit further oot of the toon."

"LAST YEAR, in Japan, I won a match under rather peculiar circumstances," said Longbow. "There was a big sum at stake and I had a putt for the match on the last green. The ball stopped on the edge of the hole, and I was about to knock it in, when a violent earthquake threw us all to the ground. On getting up we found the ball in the hole ! "

" ONE used to be able to *hear* a good player at the game," says a writer, speaking of the days of the gutta ball. One can still listen to the bad ones.

Player (in difficulties) : " What *shall* I do ? "
(After the stroke) : " Why *did* I do it ? "

AN AMERICAN once paid a great price for a mashie with which he had seen a professional make the winning stroke of an important match, but was disappointed to find that it lost most of its magic in his hands. " I guess it was not the club that won that match," he sadly said, " but the man behind it." " It was na' the club," the pro. replied, after consideration, " an' it was na' the mon. It was the *nerve*."

FROM THE BEGINNERS' COURSE :
" What have you played ? "
" One drive, two brassies, four niblicks, a jigger, a baffy, three mashies, and four putters."
" Your hole ! "

A YOUNG LADY of famous golfing family used to play a neat little game as a ten-year-old at Biarritz, where she was often to be seen tripping smartly round the course on her lonesome. One day she was following rather

M

too eagerly on the heels of the last couple out on the morning round, and drove a "screamer" of a hundred yards into a General with a reputation for putting ten adjectives to every noun. An ominous calm preceded their meeting, but the young lady got in the first word —and the last. " Fore, sir, fore ! " she cried ; " didn't you hear me call fore ? "

Beginner (after missing a six-inch putt) : "Was that me or the green ? "

"CLUBS ? " repeated the landlady with a vacant stare. " Oh, I suppose you mean that bag of old 'ockey

sticks wot you left 'ere last week. I thought as 'ow you couldn't want them dirty old things, so I put them with a bundle of cast-off clothes, and they were disposed of at the jumble sale !"

Enthusiastic Novice : " What is Braid's ' dunch ' ? "

Well-informed Man : " Braid's so busy, you see, that he has no time to take regular meals. He therefore combines lunch and dinner ! "

Novice (bunkered for the first time) : " Don't I have to throw it over my left shoulder, or something ? "

HAVING FAILED at a short putt, an irate foozler savagely struck the green and displaced a divot. The result of the afternoon match depended on this player's putt, which was deflected by the rough ground caused by his previous iniquity. "Very hard luck," remarked his opponent, who had not taken part in the morning round ; "your ball would have gone down but for that piece of rough turf. It looks as if some d——d fool had been chopping up the green !"

AN IRISHMAN had shifted his feet and waggled his club again and again, but still showed no signs of attempting to hit the ball. "What are you waiting for ?" his partner inquired. "Sure," said the other, "I can't remember all the things that I decided to forget."

AN AMERICAN professional was closely attended by his wife in an important competition. Perhaps her presence distracted the amateur marker, for he made a mistake in the score at one hole. The guardian-angel, who was looking over his shoulder, seized the card, corrected the figure, and announced, "Say, old man, I reckon *I'm* going to mark this card for the rest of this round !"

Secretary (interviewing candidate for post of professional) : "What club are you attached to at present ?"
Professional : "None in particular, sir."

Nervous Lady (whose opponent has nearly holed a long putt for the match) : " If you had gone down I should have screamed ! "

AN AMATEUR PHOTOGRAPHER, who was not a golfer,  asked permission to take one of the competitors in the Open Championship in the act of making a full drive. The professional took a swing as requested, but the snapshotter exclaimed, " That won't do. Hold your head up, please, and don't look on the ground, otherwise your face will not be seen at all ! "

BEFORE THE MATCH :
" Have another glass of sloe gin ? "
" Are you going to ? "
" Yes."
" Right, then I won't ! "

WHEN A DUFFER loses a ball from his drive, he searches on the fairway two hundred yards from the tee, his opponent searches in the rough twenty yards from the tee, and the caddie searches everywhere in the hope of finding someone else's ball.

" THE COMMITTEE have given me a handicap of
eighteen," said the elderly beginner, who was about to
play his first match with a scratch man, " so you will
have to give me a stroke a hole." "But you only
receive three-quarters of your allowance, you know,"
said the scratch player.

" Why ? " demanded the other. "Because it is one
of the rules of St. Andrews," was the reply. "Ah,"
cried the disappointed Londoner, "I had forgotten
that the game is of *Scottish* origin ! "

FOUR PLAYERS arrived at the last green to find it
occupied by an old gentleman who was staring stolidly
at the hole. One of them
at last went forward to
request him to move.
" You can't come on,"
was the reply. "I had a
four-foot putt for the
match and the ball came
to rest on the lip of the
hole exactly as you see it
now, but the wind's in

the right quarter and increasing in strength, so I'm
not going to give up for a long time yet ! "

FROM THE ADVERTISEMENTS OF A LADIES' PAPER :
" Golf : Lady's complete set of five clubs, with bag ;
Paradise lost, clean. What offers ? "

THE PRETTY GIRL, who was having a lesson, looked deeply dejected. "It's no use, McPherson," she cried, "I'm afraid I shall never make a golfer." "Naw, miss," replied the pro., "ye hae the hecht, an' ye hae the swing, but ye've nae the heid, ye ken."

THREE well-known professionals were playing an exhibition medal round on a new course. At the thirteenth A found his ball buried in a mole-hill, which cost him three strokes. This put B ahead, but at the next hole *he* found trouble in the shape of a rabbit warren in the fairway. C, who eventually won, although he had not played the best golf, was

afterwards heard to remark, "Well, I never heard such a couple of grumbling beggars in all my life!"

Foozler (after missing the ball three times): "Can you see what I'm doing, boy?" *Caddie* (who is thoroughly enjoying the fun): "Yes, thank you, sir."

"GO ON, DARLING," cried the fast young lady, as her approach putt threatened to stop very short. "Right you are, miss," said the bewildered assistant pro., "but I think it's still your turn to play."

Affable Old Lady : "Let me congratulate you, Captain ;
I hear you have won one of those *bogus* competitions ! "

FROM THE NOTICE BOARD OF AN IRISH CLUB-HOUSE :
" Members are prohibited from playing with dogs."
Every dog must *not* have his day.

Bogey Competitor (passing a slow couple of beginners) :
" Are you two playing a friendly match ? "
Senior Wrangler : " No, not very ! "

A VISITOR to Westward Ho ! was inquiring the
correct name of the water which had to be crossed at
the last hole. " Some calls it by one name and some
another," said his caddie ; " it depends on the circumstances. There's an old Scotch gentleman, and when
he gets over it he says he has carried the 'burn,' but
when he tops into it he says, ' Pick my ball out of that
d——d sewer ' ! "

WHAT POPE GREGORY might have said had he seen
the Scots at their national pursuit :
" Not skittish, but Scottish."

" How DO YOU LIKE the members of your new
Municipal Club ? "
" Oh, they're very genial. They call you 'Sir' the
first time they play with you, and 'old man' for ever
after."

Deliberate Visitor : " How long is the next hole ? "
Absent-minded Host (anxious to get home for lunch) :
" About twenty minutes, I'm afraid."

A GOLFER in the North used to employ as a caddie an
old man whose intimate knowledge of the game was
of great value.   The old fellow was not strictly
honest, however, and his employer, having one day
detected him in some small theft, said : " When you
die, Mac, you will not go to Heaven." Perhaps the
caddie did not catch the words, or it may have been
his innate sense of obedience which prompted the
meek reply, " Verra weel, sir ! "

WHEN Taylor pitched and Braid " ran,"
Which was then the better plan ?

" DID YE SEE that foine stroke Oi made whin me ball
was floatin' down the river, Patrick ? "
" Yes, an' it's disqualified ye'll be, for I saw ye
groundin' your club in the wather ! "

Captain Convert : " The misses don't count, do they ? "
Colonel Henpeck : " *Mine* does ! "

The Conquering Hero

THE front door banged importantly, heavy boots came clumping along the hall, the Master staggered into the drawing-room and subsided with an assertive sigh of satisfaction into the softness of the central sofa.

"The day of my life," he beamed ; "a red-letter day ! Never have I played such sterling golf. . . . I was in champion form ! . . . It was a regular exhibition match !" . . . .

The Mistress sat very upright, intent on her sewing.

"You didn't——"

"Yes, yes, I did," the Master broke in. "I won the Grand Championship Cup presented by our President, Count Ivan Offelitch, and valued, so I heard him say, at more than two hundred guineas. I keep it for six months only, of course, but just think how fine it will look on your silver table ! . . . Yes, I know you asked me not to bring home any more prizes because the servants object to cleaning any extra silver, but this trophy is fashioned out of solid gold, and—well, I don't mind giving it a rub over with emery paper myself now and then. As to the responsibility, I met a man to-day who is willing to insure it at reduced rates for golfers, for a sovereign or two a month. . . . You really

97   N

should have seen my play to-day. You would have been proud of me. Poor old Howker never got a sniff in the final. I was dormy four, but I so arranged it that I only won by a long putt on the last green. Doesn't do to break a fellow's heart, you know. Only a game, after all. Everybody was talking about me afterwards. You'd have blushed to hear their flattering remarks. I'd explain all about the match, only I'm afraid you wouldn't appre-

ciate the beauties of it. Pity you don't play golf! The best part of it all is to come, though. As it was a holiday some of the members thought the visitors might like to have a sweepstake in the afternoon. The Secretary made the groundsman cut new holes during lunch, and there was quite a fair number of starters considering that the entrance fee was a quid."

"You didn't——"

"Oh, yes, I really *had* to go in for it. You see, it would have seemed so unsporting of me not to enter, after winning the Cup in the morning. Besides, I was at the top of my form, and I know the course so well that I could play it blindfolded. It would have been foolhardy to chuck away a chance like that. I know you don't like me to play two full

rounds a day, but somehow I don't feel a bit tired
to-night. I was eighty-three net, and just as I came
to the last green I heard that some stranger had put in
a scratch score of seventy-nine, but what do you think
I did?"

"You didn't——"

"Tear up my card? Not much! I put it in,
and the stranger was disqualified for breaking our
local rule about dropping instead of placing his ball off
a wrong green. Served him right for not knowing
the rules, eh? My score was the next best, so here I
am a winner of something like thirty pounds! . . .
Of course I must spend the money on something to
do with golf or I should become a mere pro. at
once. I stood a bottle of fizz to the other competitors, but I haven't decided what to do with
the rest of the money yet. Perhaps I shall buy a
piece of plate as a memento, or I may join that
expensive new Club at Northsea . . . or treat myself
to a holiday at Le Touquet . . . or Biarritz. . . .
What a pity that you don't play golf!"

The Mistress glanced at the clock, gathered up her
work, and walked to the door.

"You didn't wipe your boots when you came in,"
she said; "go and do so at once."

And the Master went.

Medal Play

SCENE. *The thirteenth green at Borough-super-Mare, in a thick mist.*

First Duffer (looking round): "There! I *told* you I was over. Pretty good shot, though, eh? I ought to have taken a mashie."

Second Duffer: "Well, I don't want to lose mine, too. I'm doing rather a good score—only three over sixes. I think I'd better hole out."

(He does so, in eight.)

First Duffer (anxiously): "Can't you find it, boy? Why didn't you mark it? What do you imagine you're paid for? Where do you think it went? How can you expect to——"

Second Duffer: "Here it is. Only just ran over the green, after all, you see."

First Duffer hastens joyfully towards it.

Enter Third and Fourth Duffers.

Third Duffer: "Mine came just about here, too. Are you sure that's your ball, sir? What are you playing with?"

First Duffer (trying to read the name on the ball): "A 'Plum.'"

Third Duffer: "Well, so am I, and I know that's my ball because I recognise the——"

(An argument.)

Second Duffer: "I think you will find that's my opponent's ball, sir. He played much too strong, and the ball took just this direction."

Fourth Duffer: "But so did *my* opponent's, sir, and I'm sure it must be *his* ball, because if it had been the other's you would have found it before his came down, where-as——"

(A discussion.)

First Duffer's Caddie: "It's our ball!"

Third Duffer's Caddie: "It ain't!"

(A fight.)

Enter a Lady.

The Lady: "Oh, I'm so sorry; I didn't know you were still on the green, and I was practising mashie shots. Have you seen my ball? Ah, you have it. Thank you *so* much!"

First and Third Duffers: "Pardon me, that is *my* ball."

The Lady: "What are you playing with?"

First and Third Duffers: "A 'Plum.'"

The Lady (inspecting the ball closely): "But this is a 'Peach,' as you see. I passed a ball on the way up the hill. It is lying in a bunker a short distance back."

First and Third Duffers: "Oh, *that* will be mine, then."

The Lady: "And I saw another 'Plum' nicely tee'd up on the fairway about ten yards nearer the green."

First and Third Duffers : " Oh, thank you ! *That*
must be mine."

They return to find that two worse Duffers have come
up and taken possession of these balls, claiming them as
their own.

The fog thickens.

The Major's Bogey

"I WOULDN'T tell this story to everyone, mind you," said the Major, as he carefully closed the door, "but you know me better than to suspect that I would exaggerate on a matter of such serious importance as that which I am about to mention. The experience was so startling—so alarming—that—— But you shall judge for yourself.

"About a fortnight ago I came up here for a game, and finding the links deserted, I went round by myself with Bogey as an opponent. I was badly beaten and was disgusted to think that I could not do better with my liberal handicap. I ate a lonely lunch and afterwards strolled out on to the home green to practise short putts, several of which I had missed in the morning.

"Now, you know that I am an even-tempered man as a rule and not given to swearing more than is absolutely necessary, but when I failed to hole three out of four putts of a foot, I savagely exclaimed, 'I wish the devil I could beat Bogey!'

"'You *shall*,' said a quiet voice at my elbow.

"I turned quickly to see a stranger standing beside me. He was tall and thin, with an aquiline nose and dark close-cropped hair. There was something masterful and mysterious in the glint of his eyes. He limped.

" 'I—I beg your pardon ?' I stammered.

" 'You want to beat Bogey ?' he said. 'Very well, you shall. Follow me.'

"This must be the new professional, I thought, as I found myself obediently following him to the first teeing-ground.

"He made an enormous mound of sand, dumped the ball on the top, and told me to drive. Of course I cut right under it and sent the ball ten yards or so into a heavy lie.

" 'You evidently need a little instruction,' said the dark man, grimly : 'take your driver again, and hit the ball as hard as ever you can *on the top !*'

"I did so, and the ball, after a long straight flight, just reached the green. It was the finest stroke I ever made. I studied the putt with care and played firmly, but my 'Mono' stopped quite eight yards away from the hole.

" 'There,' I cried, 'you see I can't putt. I shall lose *this* hole, anyway.'

" 'You can't putt,' said the stranger, calmly, 'because you try too hard. Just walk straight up to it and knock it carelessly along with a pushing stroke, while you keep your eye steadily fixed *on the hole !*' Now that I was recovering from my surprise at receiving such curious advice, I began to feel indignant with this suave stranger who had volunteered to give instruction which, while violating all the precepts which I had spent a lifetime in acquiring, had nevertheless met with marvellous success. I did exactly as he told me, however, and the putt went down.

" 'One up,' said my unknown teacher, as he led the way to the next tee. He threw down the ball and, handing me a cleek, said : 'Grip hard with your right hand, loose with your left. Swing back as fast and as far as you can. Then throw your body at the ball, and *don't follow through !* '

"Again I obeyed to the best of my ability, and the ball dropped into the bunker which guards the green two hundred and fifty yards away. The stranger was annoyed.

" 'You'd have carried that comfortably,' he said, 'if only you had not kept your head so sanctimoniously still ! '

"I was really angry this time. The man must be mad, I said to myself—quite mad. He had picked up the bag and was hurrying on ahead, the clubs rattling as he limped.

" 'Look here, sir,' I cried, as I came up with him, 'are you aware that you have been recommending me to cultivate the worst of golfing *faults*, to do everything, in fact, which has always been recognised as *sinful*, and thoroughly *bad* for one's game ? '

"The strange man winced.

" 'Who has told you that these things are wrong ? ' he asked.

" 'Why, the experts,' I replied ; 'those who know, you know ; the leading professionals.'

" My instructor laughed harshly.

" ' The professionals, indeed ! And are you so simple as to suppose that they would tell you all they know ? Why do the professionals still manage to keep ahead of the best amateurs ? Because they have discovered golfing truths. But do you imagine that they would be so foolish as to give away the secrets by means of which they earn their living, only to be supplanted by their own pupils ? Certainly not. Believe me, sir, the old saws " slow back," &c., are an invention of

the dev — er — I should say a device of the professionals !' "I won that hole from Bogey.

" ' This next one is a short hole,' the stranger continued. ' Rise well up on your toes, take care to sway with your whole body, and look up *long before you strike the ball !* '

" He handed me a putter and, after I had played, I saw my ' Mono ' make straight for a big sand bunker, run through it on to the green, hit the flag-post, and disappear into the hole !

" I was so astounded at these almost miraculous events that I continued to play on as in a dream, doing exactly as I was told, until I found myself eight up at the turn.

"Even my impassive companion was by this time beginning to show signs of suppressed excitement at my marvellous play, and I noticed that he was puffing nervously at a cigar, though how he had contrived to light it was a mystery, since there was a strong wind blowing and no shelter near.

"I now began to imagine all sorts of uncanny things about this eccentric being and his methods. Could it be, I asked myself, that the accepted principles were rotten after all? No. My wonderful score must have been due to an extraordinary sequence of lucky chances. Then at last I determined to revolt from this tyranny and I began to play my own game. From that moment I lost hole after hole, but I steadily declined to avail myself of the advice which the stranger kept eagerly whispering into my ear.

"The match stood all square as I prepared to address the ball on the eighteenth teeing-ground. My companion was swearing now in some strange tongue.

"'Look here, sir,' he broke out, just as I was about to drive, 'when I promised that you should beat Bogey it was only on the understanding that you would implicitly obey all my instructions. You have not done so, but there is still a chance. This is, as you know, a Bogey four. Do as I tell you and you shall hole it in three and win the match. Crouch well down, duck your right shoulder as you hit, and *press for all you're worth*.'

"I involuntarily obeyed, and hit a screamer, but when I came up the ball was found to have settled deep in a hoof mark. I knew that my only hope was to chip out with a niblick, for I could certainly not reach the green, although it was only a mashie shot away.

"'I'm beaten now, anyway,' I exclaimed, and could hardly hide my satisfaction.

"'Beaten?' the stranger repeated. 'Not at all.' He thrust a putter into my hands. 'Jump at the ball,' he cried, 'and slam at it with one hand, aiming at the ground *a yard or two in front!*'

"This was really too much, and I completely lost my temper. Rushing at the ball, I aimed a terrific blow with one hand just where he had told me.

"I don't quite know what happened, for a huge divot hit me hard in the eye, but when I next looked up I saw that my 'Mono' had come to rest only about a foot from the hole. I hurried on to the green fuming with rage, and determined that for the winning putt at least I would not be indebted to the advice of a stranger. With great care I settled down to the stroke, and as I did so I noticed out of the corner of my eye that my companion had thrown away his cigar stump and was dancing about with excitement.

"I aimed at the centre of the ball, then played at it with confidence and—missed it altogether!

"'There!' I cried, spinning round; 'what did I tell you? I——'

"Utterly astounded, I stood staring about me.

"The stranger had disappeared !

"I ran this way and that, searching in every direction, but there was no sign of him.

"One thing I did notice, however, namely, a very strong smell of sulphur, and, do you know, after thinking the matter over very seriously, I have been forced to the conclusion that this person must have been a dev——"

The Major paused with his glass half raised in his hand. He turned pale. His mouth dropped open and his eyes gazed fixedly at the door. I looked round sharply and saw a tall dark man standing in the entrance.

"Why, Professor," I exclaimed, "I didn't know you had arrived. I heard you had taken a house here for the winter, and I thought we should have seen you on the links before this."

"I came up one day about a fortnight ago," the new-comer answered, "and I had the pleasure of walking round with this gentleman ; but we have not been formally introduced."

"Major," said I, "allow me to introduce Professor Brayne, Lecturer in Oriental Languages to the University."

The Major bowed in silence.

"I'm afraid you must have thought me very rude to leave you so abruptly the other day," said the Professor, "and I feel that I owe you an explanation. I was so much excited to see the finish of your game that I absent-mindedly put my lighted cigar-end into the pocket where I was carrying some loose fusees. They immediately flared up, and in my alarm I started to run. It seemed to me that my best course was to make for the water, so I set out for the sea across the sand dunes as fast as my game leg would carry me. I plunged straight into the waves, and I have no doubt that this saved my life. As it was, I suffered rather severely from burns and have been laid up ever since. I have nearly recovered now, however, and came up in the hope of finding you in order to offer an apology."

" Thanks," said the Major, who seemed slightly dazed ; " but I still don't understand by what strange power you caused me to go out in a score of which the champion himself might have been proud."

" Well," said the Professor, smiling, " my chief hobby is the study of golf in all its intricacies. One of my latest theories is that our difficulties are mostly of our own making, and I took the liberty of subjecting you to some interesting experiments which, you must confess, showed remarkable results. Of course I had to exaggerate my views in order to put them fully to the test, but, aided by what can only have been an exceptional run of luck, I succeeded beyond all my expectations. I hope you will forgive me."

"With all my heart," the Major replied. " I have since tried to benefit by your instructions, but naturally I have not repeated these miracles. You have, how-

ever, taught me a valuable lesson, namely, that one
may nullify all one's labours by taking too much care.
Thanks to you, my game has improved enormously,
and I was just remarking as you came in that I
consider you to be a dev—— er—a decidedly clever
teacher. I am proud to have made your acquaintance,
Professor."

The men shook hands.

A Golfer's Waits and Measures

$5\frac{9}{10}$ inches make one stymie.

3 stymies make one dam.

1760 dams make one wince.

Yarn Measure.

20 grains of salt make one scruple.

2 scruples make one hesitate.

Avoirdupois Wait.

24 stone make one fat man.

2 fat men make one hundred wait.

Golfing Geometry.

DEFINITIONS :

A *line* is that which is asked for by the player, given by the caddie, and not taken by the ball.

A *squared* match is one in which all the sides are square at the end of the round.

A *good partner* is one who has length, breadth of mind, but no weakness.

A *point* is that which is arrived at in one (or more) strokes.

A *dameter* is a species of gramophone affixed to certain bunkers whereby the players' feelings may be expressed in terms whose strength is regulated by the sum which is deposited in the machine.

A *theorem* is a proposition whose object is to air the views of its exponent by inducing a newspaper controversy.

A *problem* is a proposition whose object is prematurely to hasten the Rules of Golf Committee into a retreat for those of unsound mind.

EXPOSTULATES :

Let it be granted,

That a line must be drawn somewhere, when the credulity of the hearers has been stretched to its utmost capacity.

That a " remarkable incident " may be described at any date and without any data, as having occurred at any time and place.

A LAXIOM is a self-asserting truth which neither requires nor is capable of proof, but which serves as a foundation for future argument.

Example : "When I was playing alone this morning I did the long hole in one," &c.

GENERAL LAXIOMS.

Things which come to the same thing are the same thing as one another.

Example : "I did a record round ; I didn't hole out on some of the greens, but I was practically dead."

The hole is smaller than the ball.

The Rules—Revised

A "SIDE" consists either of one player or of two players.

"Side" is often put on, however, by any number of players.

"Advice" is any counsel or suggestion which could influence a player . . . in the method of making a stroke.

"You'd better not drive into us" is not advice. It is threat.

Casual water" is any temporary accumulation of water —undiluted with whisky.

"Out of bounds" is all ground on which play is prohibited.

The whole course is usually out of bounds on Sundays.

The hole shall be $4\frac{1}{4}$ inches in diameter.

But shall never look so much.

In "teeing," the ball may be placed on the ground, or on sand, or other substance.

Such as a gold watch.

"You'd better not drive into us" is not
advice.   It is a threat.

A ball is deemed to "move" if it leave its original position.
If its original position was the pocket of a golf bag, it may be deemed to have been *re*moved.

The reckoning of strokes is kept by the terms—"the odd" . . .
The *very* odd, &c.

A single player has no standing.
But if there is a fast couple behind, he may have quite a lot of running.

If a player's ball strike an opponent . . . the opponent shall lose the match.
And the player will probably lose the opponent.

If a ball be completely covered by sand, only so much thereof may be removed as will enable the player to see the top of his ball.
If the top of the ball is found to be situated at the bottom, extensive excavations may become necessary.

A competitor shall not waive any penalty.
It is advisable not to wave anything at all.

When one player plays his ball against the better ball of two other players, the match is called a best-ball match.
No matter how bad the best ball may be.

When two players play their better ball against the better ball of two other players, the match is called a four-ball match.

It is occasionally called by other names.

On the putting green the stroke may be recalled by an opponent . . .

It may be, and often is, recalled in the Club House by the player.

A Golfer's Cursory Rhymes

THERE was an old duffer who lived in a stew;
He read so many books he didn't know what to do.
He tried to remember what each one had said,
But the sight of the ball drove it out of his head.

ISOLATION is vexation,
A twosome's just as bad,
A game of three does puzzle me,
And four-balls drive me mad!

OLD Muddle-head could ne'er get dead,
His partner could not drive
One ball in three, and so, you see,
They kept the game alive.

I HAD a Schenectady,
But, on an evil day,
I lent it to a lady
Who was learning how to play.

She thought it was a driver
And broke it clean in twain.
I would not for a fiver
Lend out a club again.

FORE! *Fore!!* Lor', what a bore!
Slowman's a regular blaster ;
He ought to play only nine holes a day,
Because he won't walk any faster.

" WHERE are you going to, my pretty jade ? "
" I'm going a-golfing, sir," she said.
" May I go with you, my pretty jade ? "
" That would be toppin', sir," she said.
" What is your father, my pretty jade ? "
" Millionaire pork-butcher, sir," she said.
" What is your handicap, my
    pretty jade ? "
" My temper's my handicap,
    sir," she said.
" Then I fear I can't play with
    you, my pretty jade."
" Nobody will, worse luck,"
    she said.

" TWINKLE, twinkle, little baa',
How I wonder waur ye are.
Maybe, since ye went sae high,
Ye'll be bunkered in the sky ? "

    " OH, go ahead," cried Forcing Fred.
        " Tarry awhile," said Slow.
    " They've both played two," said Hasty Hugh,
        " I'll just shout 'Fore,' and go ! "

Q

I saw a ball a-sailing, a-sailing out of bounds ;
That slice o' mine's a failing that costs me
        pounds and pounds.

Pat-a-cake, pat-a-cake, my little man,
Bring me some sand as quick as you can ;
Pinch it and pat it and make a high tee,
Then stand aside and see what you shall see.

        Little Bo-peep
        Has lost her sheep,
        But doesn't seem to mind them.
        Leave them alone
        And they'll come home ;
        The *golfers* are sure to "find" them.

"Jonathan, Jonathan, where have you been ?"
"I've been to visit a classical green."
"Jonathan, Jonathan, what did you there ?"
"I played in pyjamas, and *didn't* they stare ?"

        Hush-a-bye, "Baby," on the tee top,
        Over the bunkers you gaily shall hop,
        Into the hole in one stroke you shall fall,
        Down will come handicap, Bogey, and all.

A golfer once holed out in nothing at all,
A score that you'll grant is sufficiently small.
You'd "very much like to know how it was done ?"
A stroke hole, you see, and he did it in one !

"WHERE have you been all the day with that
  Sammy ? "
    " I've been all the day
     Trying to improve my play,
     But I've spoilt it—damme ! "

  SOLOMON GRUNDY despised golf on Monday,
  Tried it on Tuesday,
  Played it all Wednesday,
  Took lessons on Thursday,
  Got a handicap Friday,
  Won the Medal on Saturday,
  Grumbled all Sunday . . .
  That's the beginning of Solomon Grundy.

RUB-a-dub-dub,
The worst men in the Club ;
 And who do you think they
  be ?
The " maker," the faker,
The etiquette-breaker ;
 Show 'em up, knaves all three.

"ONE . . . two . . . three,
 four, five ;
(Now to hole out I must strive)
Six, seven, eight, nine, ten . . .
(Dammit, I'll begin again !) "

As I was waiting on the links,
I met a man who had ten drinks.
He'd had *ten* drinks and I'd had none . . .
He only beat me three and one.

HEY diddle diddle,
The rough and the middle,
The man, and the maid, and the "spoon."
The caddie boy laughed to see such sport,
And the couple decided that a crowded holiday golf
    resort was hardly an ideal spot in which to spend
    their honeymoon.

IF I won a sweepstake—a good fat sweepstake—
(I love a sweepstake better than my life),
I'd stand a drink or two,
But I would not—would you?—
Take back a bally sou
Home to my wife.

"LADY-BIRD, Lady-bird, fly away home;
Your house is on fire and your children alone."
"Wait a bit, wait a bit; sh! not a sound.
If I hole this short putt I'll have done a good
    round!"

Go for the pin if you're anxious to win;
You will never go "out" if you cannot get in.

"HIGGLEDY, piggledy, my fine men,
Lay out ze links for shentlemen.
If zey play 'ere every day,
Ze Grand Hotel will pay its way ! "

THERE was a jolly miller
Who didn't care a d——.
He duffed and fluffed from morn till night,
No lark so blithe as he.
And this the burden of his song
For ever used to be :
"I'll play with nobody, no, not I,
For no one'll play with me ! "

ONE misty, moisty morning,
When foggy was the weather,
There I met an old man,
And we played together.

And we played together,
In the fog and rain.
I lost him and he lost me . . .
We never met again.

MARY had a little ball,
It *did* annoy her so,
For everywhere that Mary meant
That ball declined to go.

" PETER, Peter, best green keeper,
How does your fairway grow ? "
"I cut, and roll, and mow, and cut,
And roll, and cut, and mow ! "

" BAA, Baa, black sheep, have you won a ball ? "
" Yes, sir, yes, sir, quite a good haul ;
One from a blind man, and one from a lame,
But none from the old Scot who understands the
    game."

HERE am I, little Bouncing Billy,
When I bump on the green, I make men look silly.

THERE was an old duffer, as I've heard tell,
Who hit very often, but not very well.
He couldn't play golf, but I've heard people say
That he hadn't an equal at making the hay.

THE North Wind doth blow,
And we shall have snow,
And what will old Crabbie do then, poor thing ?
He'll mope in his house
And will grumble and grouse,
And make his wife study his swing—*poor* thing !

The Three Jovial Golfers

IT'S of three jovial golfers, and a-golfing they did go,
   An' they foozled an' they fumbled, for they
couldn't play a blow.
   Look ye there !

They foozled an' they fumbled, an' the first thing they
   did find
Was a big new-fashioned bunker, which didn't prove
   too kind.
One said " That *is* a bunker !" but another he said
   " Nay,
It's an imitation sand dune, composed of London
   clay ! "
   Look ye there !

They fumbled an' they foozled, an' the next hole they
   did find
Was a full six hundred yarder, an' most of it was
   blind.
One said it was a bad hole, but another he said " Nay,
It's not the *hole* that's bad, old ' Hit-and-chance-it,'—
   it's the *play !* "
   Look ye there !

They foozled an' they fumbled, an' the next thing they
did find
Was a brand-new half-crown golf-ball, and *that* they
left behind.
One thought it was a golf-ball, but another he said
"Nay,
It's but a bally puff-ball!"—and smacked it clean
away!
Look ye there!

They foozled an' they fumbled, an' the next thing they
did find
Was a most insistent party a-shouting "Fore!"
behind.
One said "They'd better pass us," but another he said
"Nay,
It's nothing but a four-ball; we've as much right here
as they."
Look ye there!

They foozled an' they fumbled, an' the next thing
they did find
Was a big red bunting golf-flag, a-flapping in the
wind.
One said it was a golf-flag, but another he said
"Nay,
It's the Territorial rifle range's signal; come away!"
Look ye there!

One thought it was a golf-ball, but
another he said " Nay."

So they foozled an' they fumbled, an' when the round
    was done,
Said each unto the other, " Well, *hasn't* it been fun ?
We've fumbled an' we've foozled, but we've had a
    jolly day.
Three cheers for all keen golfers—All together !—
    ' Hip, hooray !' "